BALTHASAR'S *TRILOGY*

T&T Clark *Reader's Guides* are clear, concise and accessible introductions to key texts in theology. Each book explores the themes, context, criticism and influence of key works, providing a practical introduction to close reading, guiding students towards a thorough understanding of the text. They provide an essential, up-to-date resource, ideal for undergraduate students.

Published in the series:

Aquinas' Summa Theologiae – Stephen J. Loughlin

Forthcoming in the series:

Barth's Commentary on Romans – Donald Wood
Kierkegaard's Philosophical Fragments – Tim Rose
Bonhoeffer's Ethics – Philip Ziegler
Schleiermacher's Speeches on Religion – Kevin Hector

BALTHASAR'S *TRILOGY*

A Reader's Guide

STEPHEN WIGLEY

continuum

Published by T&T Clark International
A Continuum Imprint
The Tower Building   80 Maiden Lane
11 York Road   Suite 704
London SE1 7NX   New York, NY 10038

www.continuumbooks.com

British Library Cataloguing-in-Publication Data
A catalogue record for this book is available from the British Library.

ISBN: HB: 978-0-567-03416-8
       PB: 978-0-567-03417-5

Typeset by Newgen Imaging Systems Pvt Ltd, Chennai, India
Printed and bound in India by Replika Press Pvt Ltd

CONTENTS

CONTENTS

ACKNOWLEDGEMENTS

Von Balthasar famously said that he wanted to offer a 'kneeling, not a sitting theology'. In offering this short guide to his major theological trilogy, I am conscious of writing it from the perspective not of an academic theologian, but of a church minister, albeit a pastor and preacher in a very different Methodist tradition to his own Catholic background. It also means that I am thankful for the support of my colleagues in the Wales Synod who have borne with me while this project has come to fruition over these last two years. Some parts of it, in particular the opening sections of Chapters 3 and 4, were published in an earlier form in *Karl Barth and Hans Urs von Balthasar: A Critical Engagement* (London/New York: T&T Clark International, 2007). I am grateful to Ignatius Press for permission to quote from von Balthasar's *Theo-Drama*, Volumes I–V, translated by Graham Harrison (San Francisco: Ignatius Press, 1988–98) and *Theo-Logic*, Volumes I – III, translated by Adrian J. Walker (San Francisco: Ignatius Press, 2000–05) in Chapters 4 and 5, pages 73–142. I am also grateful to Tom Kraft of Continuum/T&T Clark for first suggesting this book to me and encouraging me to write it, to Prof. Frances Young for continuing to remind me that such work is just as much a part of being a church leader as chairing Synod meetings, to my PA Judy for her help in printing off copies of the various early drafts and to Richard Hall of our Wales Training Network for looking over them and offering his comments. Above all I offer my grateful thanks to Jenny, David and Andrew who have lived with this undertaking for much of the last two years, whether fully aware of it or not, and who have shown in our family life together the truth of which von Balthasar wrote, that it is 'love alone' which is 'the way of revelation.'

Cardiff, St. Stephen's Day, 2009

ABBREVIATIONS

ET   *English Translation*

Von Balthasar's *Trilogy*

GL(1–7)   *The Glory of the Lord: A Theological Aesthetics,*
            vols 1–7
TD(1–5)   *Theo-Drama: Theological Dramatic Theory,*
            vols 1–5
TL(1–3)   *Theo-Logic,* vols 1–3

Other works by Hans Urs von Balthasar

EP   *Epilogue*
FG   *First Glance at Adrienne von Speyr*
KB   *The Theology of Karl Barth: Exposition and*
            Interpretation
LA   *Love Alone: The Way of Revelation*
MP   *Mysterium Paschale: The Mystery of Easter*

CHAPTER 1

CONTEXT AND INTRODUCTION

INTRODUCTION

Hans Urs von Balthasar (1905–1988) is one of the most significant and challenging of twentieth-century theologians. His work has been highly influential within the Catholic Church, not least through the influence of the journal *Communio: International Catholic Review* which he co-founded with, among others, Cardinal Joseph Ratzinger, now Pope Benedict XVI; yet much of it is influenced by his encounter with and study of the great Protestant theologian Karl Barth. In his recovery of the importance of aesthetics von Balthasar engages with the world of classical philosophy and the great patristic scholars; but he also goes on to engage with contemporary theologians and to develop a theological narrative and model for interpreting the Bible which is both new and distinctive. His theology is at the same time both christocentric in focus and highly ecclesial in consequence. And his extensive writings, many of which were first published by his own publishing house Johannes Verlag in Einsiedeln, reach their climax with his great trilogy beginning with *The Glory of the Lord*, followed by the *Theo-Drama* and concluding with the *Theo-Logic*.

This *magnum opus*, representing arguably the masterpiece of twentieth-century Catholic theology, is also something of a paradox, in that it is has been hugely influential and yet is not always easy to read or approach. In part, this is because of its huge size and scale, comprising some 15 volumes or 10,000 pages written over a period of nearly 30 years between 1961 and 1987. It is also to do with the panoramic vision which underpins it. The *Trilogy* is a work which was conceived and written over decades but its subject matter is the thought of centuries even millennia, engaging not just with theology but with philosophy, literature, art and culture so that its author appears equally at home in the world of Greek philosophy as he is with contemporary biblical scholarship. And finally, it is to do with the very distinctive perspective of its author, who in arriving at his distinctive and panoramic perspective, then puts his own characteristic shape and structure on the work so that it has a particular and quite unique narrative framework.

All of this means that von Balthasar's trilogy is not always an easy work to approach, a factor noted in a recent introduction to his theology, Rodney Howsare's *Balthasar: A Guide for the Perplexed.* Not only does von Balthasar write so much and in a way which makes it hard to fit him into any of the standard 'schools' of theology; he also 'makes enormous demands on his reader, both in terms of the density of his arguments and in terms of what he expects them already to know' (Howsare 2009: ix).

So why does his trilogy matter and what difference does it make to someone who seeks seriously to engage with his theology? Well, in the first place, it is written from the perspective that it is only in the encounter with the glory of God, in all Christ's divine beauty and splendour, that we discover what it means to be human beings made in the image and knowledge of God. Secondly, that it is only in the light of our being touched and transformed by the glory of God that we can be taken up into Christ's story and so become part of God's great drama of salvation seeking to redeem and restore the world. And finally it is von Balthasar's conviction that this search for the glory of God is what lies at the heart of all human endeavour and search for truth, so that what is told in the Bible and proclaimed by the Church is at one with the human quest for meaning in all times and places, part of that great narrative in which we all discover our role and find we have an important part to play.

This book is offered in the recognition that however worthwhile the effort may be, in the long run reading the trilogy will be a difficult and potentially disheartening task if undertaken without help, without some sense of how that structure is arrived at and what influences have serve to shape it. So, what this short guide seeks to do is set out the context for his great trilogy and identify some of the key themes and influences which have acted upon it. It will show how von Balthasar's reworking of theology around the transcendentals of being, the beautiful, the good and the true, is influenced not just by classical philosophy and theology but also by his involvement and relationship with such contemporaries as Henri de Lubac, Erich Przywara, Karl Barth and Adrienne von Speyr.

Inevitably, such a short guide cannot do justice to the fullness and richness of von Balthasar's vision. We shall finish with a reflection on how this work has been received and read in recent years along with a summary of some of his other writings and some pointers to more detailed and critical studies of his theology. If this introduction serves to encourage the reader to pick up a volume of say, *The Glory of the Lord*, and catch some sense of von Balthasar's wonder at the beauty of God and joy in God's presence, then it will have served its purpose.

1.1 HIS LIFE AND TIMES

Hans Urs von Balthasar was born in Lucerne in Switzerland to a prosperous and distinguished Catholic family.[1] His father, Oscar, was the canton builder, responsible among other things for building the St Karli-Kirche, one of the pioneer modern church buildings in Switzerland, while his mother, Gabrielle was co-founder and first secretary of the Swiss League of Catholic Women. Both his younger brother Dieter and sister Renée were to serve the Catholic Church, respectively as an officer in the Swiss Guard and as Superior General of the Franciscan Sisters of Sainte-Marie des Anges. So there is a sense in which his background and education might be held to have predicted his subsequent church and theological career. But a deeper study will discover that even this relatively conventional upbringing contained some significant moments of decision and pointers towards those themes which would come to life in his theological writings.

Initially the young von Balthasar attended the Benedictine high school at Engelberg which, with its opportunities for participation in orchestral masses and concerts, suited his already considerable musical gifts. Subsequently, and for reasons which have never been made clear, he and a few friends decided to transfer to the much less musically attuned Jesuit college at Feldkirche in nearby (and war-torn) Germany for the last two and a half years of high school, only to leave this school early as well, in order to matriculate secretly and begin a course in German studies at university in Zurich. These studies were to lead to a doctorate submitted to, of all places, the Liberal Protestant University of Zurich in 1928. He passed *summa cum laude* and his thesis was published in 1929 as the *History of the Eschatological Problem in Modern German Literature.* In light of his distinguished theological career thereafter, it is worth noting that his initial academic qualification was in Germanic studies rather than theology, and that for all the subsequent books he would write and honorary degrees he would be given, it was in this subject and not in theology that he would be awarded a doctorate.

In the meantime, other significant developments had taken place in his life. Despite all the distractions available to him as to any other young man of his time, he had retained throughout high school a lively Catholic faith supported by regular attendance at mass. In the summer of 1927, some time before completing his dissertation, this faith led him to undertake a 30-day retreat led by Fr. Friedrich Consider, S. J., in the Black Forest near Basel. It was while away on this retreat that, 'struck as by lightning', von Balthasar experienced his call to priesthood. Indeed some 30 years later he could still recall the precise tree and path in the forest where this call came suddenly upon him (Schindler 1991: 11). And so it was some two years later, after the completion of his dissertation and following the premature and painful death of his mother, that he entered the novitiate of the south German province of the Jesuits in November 1929.

His training followed the then normal pattern of formation for the Society of Jesus; two years in the novitiate, two (rather than three) years of philosophy at Pullach near Munich and then four years of theology at Fourvière near Lyons, which concluded with a double license in philosophy and theology. For a young man with von Balthasar's lively literary and cultural interests it was a hard and challenging time. He wrote later of his growing sense of frustration with the dryness of the neo-scholasticism that constituted his theological training during this period; what he later called 'a grim struggle with the dreariness of theology, with what men had made out of the glory of revelation' (Schindler 1991: 13). But fortunately, he also discovered the friendship of colleagues whose insights were to support him and lead him towards a very different way of approaching theology.

There were two such colleagues who would have a particular influence on his development during this period. At the house at Fourvière, von Balthasar met his great friend and inspiration Henri de Lubac. Although von Lubac never actually taught von Balthasar, he did introduce him to the Church Fathers and made available his own notes and writings. This meant, as von Balthasar himself later recalled, that, 'while all the others went off to play football, Daniélou, Bouillard, and I and a few others . . . got down to Origen, Gregory of Nyssa and Maximus' (Schindler 1991: 13). Later again, when he returned to Munich to finish working on the *Apokalypse*, the book arising from his doctoral study, he met up once more with Erich Przywara who had been one of his mentors while studying at Pullach. He was then to stay with Przywara for two years after completing his studies in 1937, working on the journal *Stimmen der Zeit* (while also completing some of his own initial writings). If it was de Lubac who helped von Balthasar to appreciate the world of the Fathers, then it was Przywara who opened von Balthasar's eyes to the way in which Catholic philosophy could engage with the contemporary world. This was to be increasingly significant just as the Catholic Church, and indeed Europe as a whole, was entering a time of profound challenge and uncertainty as the threat of war drew ever closer.

In the meantime, von Balthasar had been ordained priest by Cardinal Faulhaber in July 1936 and, after his two years in Munich, he returned to Pullach in 1939 to undertake his tertianship and to make another 30-day retreat. Following this, his training completed and against the background of the outbreak of war, came the question of what he was to do. His superiors offered him two choices: to go to Rome as a professor at the Gregorian University (to work perhaps with three other colleagues to set up an institute for ecumenical theology) or to return to Basel as a student Chaplain. Crucially and significantly, von Balthasar chose the latter and returned to Switzerland.

At this time in Switzerland, there still remained a prohibition against the formal ministry of the Jesuits in terms of work in the Church or with schools. The work to which von Balthasar and his colleagues were committed was thus one of a much more informal and personal nature, and one to which his gifts in particular were well suited. There were three areas of activity in which he was particularly engaged. The first was in writing and publishing. With the declaration of war, the German speaking Catholic community felt the increasing danger of being isolated and in response there was a conscious effort to preserve something of Europe's cultural (and Catholic) heritage. Von Balthasar was heavily involved in this enterprise through the 'European series' of the Klosterberg collection, a series of 50 short anthologies of some of Germany's finest thinkers. Von Balthasar was responsible for ten of them, including volumes on Goethe, Novalis, Nietzsche, Brentano and Borchardt. He also translated the writings of leading French intellectuals, including Claudel and Péguy, then later Bernanos and Mauriac. It was also during this period that the first of his own writings on the Fathers started to come out, beginning with his studies of Origen, Gregory and Maximus the Confessor.

At the same time, he was also heavily involved in the student-related cultural societies which abounded not just in Basel but also Zurich, Bern and Freiburg. He gave frequent lectures and was a senior member of the prominent *Akademische Gesellschaft Renaissance*. In 1941 he worked with his colleagues to found the *Studentische Schulungsgemeinschaft* which aimed to provide students with training in the philosophy of life. All these activities were supported by a network of relationships with individual students and by his leading of regular retreats in the Ignatian tradition, a pattern which eventually became open to women as well as men. Von Balthasar was a striking and charismatic figure with a wide-ranging and remarkable intellect and a gift for close friendship. All this, together with his musical gifts which enlivened many a student gathering, meant that he was to have a profound influence on the groups of young men and women who met around him, many of whom, like his close friend Robert Rast, were to find their way into the Jesuit order.

It also meant that he was to develop something of a reputation as a maker of converts to the Catholic faith – and one of the early converts was to have a profound effect on his own life. Adrienne von Speyr was a medical doctor who had married the Basel historian Emil Durr and then, following his tragic and accidental death, married his successor Professor Werner Kaegi with whom she lived at their house *Auf Burg* on the Münsterplatz in Basel until her death in 1967. The death of her first husband had been a real shock to Adrienne's faith and raised a number of questions about faith and relationships which she had experienced since childhood. It was following a series of meetings with the new Jesuit chaplain that, together with another prominent Basel academic, Professor Albert Béguin, she was prepared for and received into the Catholic faith in November 1940.

Such high profile conversions caused something of a stir in the closely-knit Protestant and academic community in Basel. They also started to raise eyebrows within Catholic circles as von Balthasar came to spend an increasing about of time as her spiritual director. Stories started to emerge of the visions which Adrienne apparently had seen and the miracles she had experienced, all of which were to be written down and recorded by von Balthasar. These stories coincided with a growing and joint commitment to explore the idea of a new 'secular' order of Christian discipleship. This idea bore fruit with the establishment of the Community of St John, initially with three women postulants, in October 1945. As questions continued to be raised about the official status of Adrienne's visions, the two decided to found their own publishing house, the Johannes Verlag, in Einsiedeln in 1947 to avoid growing difficulties about obtaining the Catholic imprimatur for publishing Adrienne's work. It was the Johannes Verlag which would go on to publish not only much of von Balthasar's work but also many volumes of Adrienne's writings, not least her commentaries on John's Gospel and Revelation.

At the same time there was another and very different friendship developing which would have a critical impact on von Balthasar's life and theology. This was with the great Protestant theologian Karl Barth who had come to Basel following his ejection from his Chair at Bonn by the Nazi authorities. Von Balthasar had already been introduced to Barth's thought by his mentor Przywara; now that they were to some degree 'colleagues' in Basel, a real ecumenical friendship developed, nurtured by a shared love of music, especially the music of Mozart. Initially von Balthasar was encouraged to sit in on some of Barth's seminars with his students. This led to an invitation for von Balthasar himself to prepare a series of papers on Barth's theology and all of this resulted in von Balthasar's seminal study *The Theology of Karl Barth* published in 1951. This study was the first major engagement with Barth's theology from the perspective of a Catholic theologian, and it was to have a major impact on subsequent interpretation of his work, not least as it appeared to have a degree of appreciation and approval from the great man himself (although as we shall note later, there remained some substantial areas of disagreement between the two).

However, at the same time as this ecumenical relationship was developing, his relationship with his own Catholic superiors was getting increasingly problematical. These tensions were heightened by the fact that at the same time von Balthasar was having to cope with a number of pressing personal and family problems throughout this period. His father died after a long illness in June 1946 and this death was followed by his godmother, to whom he was very close, suffering a stroke which left her paralysed. His young friend Robert Rast died tragically in May 1946 while von Balthasar was trying to arrange care and a visa permit to Switzerland for his mentor Erich Przywara who had suffered a nervous breakdown. But at the heart of the issues he had to face was the concern over his relationship with Adrienne von Speyr, and questions both about the validity of her religious experiences and their joint commitment to the Society of St John for which his own order, the Society of Jesus, refused to take responsibility.

This growing crisis came to a head with the requirement that von Balthasar make his solemn religious profession before his Jesuit superiors in the August of 1946. Von Balthasar asked that an investigation be made into Adrienne's visions and that his own vows be postponed until this was undertaken. There followed a series of meeting with his Jesuit superiors in 1947 before von Balthasar went away on a directed retreat in 1948 to reflect on his final decision. His prayerful but painful decision following the retreat was to leave the Society, if it was not willing to support him in testing that mission which he had developed jointly with Adrienne. There then followed some 18 months in which friends and colleagues tried frantically to see if any other way could be found to resolve this impasse – but there was not. And so on 11 February 1950 von Balthasar left the Society of Jesus.

This decision was a momentous one for von Balthasar's faith and theology, not least in terms of the emphasis he had always placed while leading retreats on the Ignatian understanding of obedience. It was not one made lightly. In a letter to the colleagues he was leaving, he wrote:

> I took this step, for both sides a very grave one, after a long testing of the certainty I had reached through prayer that I was being called by God to certain definite tasks in the Church. The Society felt it could not release me to give these tasks my undivided commitment . . . So, for me, the step taken means an application of Christian obedience to God, who at any time has the right to call a man not only out of his physical home or his marriage, but also from his chosen spiritual home in a religious order, so that he can use him for his purposes within the Church. (Schindler 1991: 21)

It was also a critical one in terms of how von Balthasar was to live and support himself. Initially an apartment was found for him outside Basel and a limited ecclesiastical permission was obtained for him to say mass and hear confessions in order that he could lead retreats. But it was not until February 1956 that he was formally incardinated or licensed in the diocese of Chur and was then able to move back to Basel to accept the hospitality of the Kaegis' and live in their house in the Münsterplatz. Financially he had to survive by repeatedly undertaking lecture tours across Germany and leading retreats. At the same time, he was also having to cope with Adrienne's increasing illnesses. Her health had grown worse even as her spiritual insights deepened, so that not only did she have to withdraw from medical practice but from 1954 was unable even to leave her own house. All this had consequences for von Balthasar's health, which started to deteriorate from 1957 onwards, affected first by exhaustion, followed by phlebitis and then by the onset of a form of leukaemia.

Yet despite all this, he managed to keep working, especially writing. Indeed, it was during this period that the initial planning for his great trilogy started to emerge. He wrote towards the end of 1958 that, 'I am trying to bring aesthetics and theology face to face. This is my first attempt at the high peaks. A tremendous theme, but who would be up to it these days?' (Schindler 1991: 27) It was a fair question to ask, but von Balthasar remained dedicated to the task. In one sense, his relative isolation from the rest of the Church helped him, in that he was not invited to the proceedings of the recalled Vatican Council, and thus was able to concentrate more on his own work. In time the first volume of his *Theological Aesthetics, Seeing the Form*, was duly published by Johannes Verlag in 1961, with the remaining six volumes to be published over the next eight years.

However, before this first part of the trilogy could be completed, Adrienne had passed away. She had been in poor health for years and was almost blind for the last three years of her life before dying an agonisingly slow death from cancer of the bowel in September 1967. For von Balthasar, her death was an immense and painful loss. He devoted himself to the private printing of her unpublished works and wrote that, 'Her work and mine cannot be separated from one another either psychologically or theologically. They are two halves of one whole with a single foundation at the centre' (Schindler 1991: 28). Yet paradoxically, it was her death which helped to begin the slow process of his reintegration into the centre of Catholic life and theology. For on the one hand, it freed him up to pursue his theological writings without the pressure of attending to and writing up Adrienne's mystical experiences. And at the same time, it freed the Catholic authorities, in Adrienne's absence, to renew the relationship and to appreciate the very real gifts which this eminently Catholic theologian could bring to the life of the Church.

So it was that the last 20 years of his life were to prove an extraordinarily fruitful time in terms of his theological writing and reception, with first the completion of the final volume of his *Theological Aesthetics* in 1969, then the five volumes of the *Theo-Drama* between 1973–1983 and finally the three volumes of his *Theo-Logic* between 1985–1987. Throughout this period, and as the initial enthusiasm for the reforms of the Vatican Council started to wear thin, von Balthasar's work and reputation stared to have an increasing appeal among more traditional circles within the Vatican. As one well-informed commentator has written, 'Separated from Adrienne . . . his intellectual stature increasingly self-evident, he was exactly the kind of anti-liberal but reforming theologian, neo-patristic in his sympathies, with whom the Roman see in the later years of Paul VI's pontificate and that of John Paul II, liked to do business' (Nichols 2000: xix).

Having not been present at meetings of the Council itself, he was in 1969 appointed a founding member of the Pope's

International Theological Commission which followed it, then a theological secretary at the second Synod of Bishops in 1971. Together with some other colleagues on the Commission (including Cardinal Ratzinger, later to become Pope Benedict XVI) he went on to found the journal, *Communio: International Catholic Review* in 1973, a journal which offered a very different viewpoint on Catholic teaching to the journal *Concilium*, one of the fruits of the Council. He received a growing number of awards and honorary degrees; the Romano Guardini Prize from the Catholic Academy of Bavaria in 1971, a Corresponding Fellowship of the British Academy in 1973 and an *Associé Étranger* of the French Academy in 1975. In 1984 he received perhaps his highest honour, the International Pope Paul VI Prize from the hands of the Pope himself. This was followed in 1987 by an award which, in view of his lifelong love of music, was perhaps equally dear to his heart, namely the Wolfgang Amadeus Mozart Prize in Innsbruck.

However, for all this process of honouring and reinstating, there remained one matter outstanding. Towards the very end of his life he heard the news that he was to be appointed a Cardinal. He returned reluctantly to Rome to prepare for the honour and be fitted for the occasion, but his request for readmission to the Society of Jesus could not be accepted because of his insistence that this should also include the Order taking responsibility for the Community of St John. For similar reasons, the Father General was unable to offer him the ancient church of Sant' Ignazio in Rome as a titular church. And so when von Balthasar died quietly, while preparing to celebrate mass on 26 June 1988, just two days before his elevation as a cardinal, for all the honour and approbation which he had received from the Church the fundamental issue which had led to his leaving the Jesuit order remained unresolved.

Perhaps it is right that this irresolution remained; because for all the conventionally Catholic nature of his upbringing and training, it is noticeable that many of the key decisions and relationships which would most influence his work took place when he was consciously (and sometimes critically) on the boundaries and outside of the mainstream of Catholic thought. We have noted the significance of his initial academic background in Germanic studies rather than theology; his sense of frustration at the formal training theological he received from the Society of Jesus and at the same time the importance of two fellow Jesuit mentors from this period in Henri de Lubac and Erich Przywara; then the unease aroused by his relationship with Adrienne von Speyr and their joint attempt to establish a secular order; and how, while all this was happening, von Balthasar was beginning a lifelong friendship with the great Protestant theologian Karl Barth who was also to have a critical influence on the shape and structure of his subsequent theology.

All this helps to remind us that while von Balthasar is unmistakably a Catholic theologian, he is in no sense a conventional or conformist one. It also begins to explain why it is that his great theological trilogy takes on the particular and characteristic shape that it does. And so, before we go on to explore the particular structure of this work, it is perhaps worth taking note of how these specific people and relationships serve to influence his thought.

CHAPTER 2

KEY INFLUENCES ON
VON BALTHASAR'S *TRILOGY*

Such is the size and scale of von Balthasar's trilogy that it may seem an impossible task to try to identify what are the key influences on his work. After all, this is a man whom his friend Henri de Lubac once described as 'perhaps the most cultivated of his time', going on to state how,

> If there is a Christian culture, then here it is! Classical antiquity, the great European literatures, the metaphysical tradition, the history of religions, the diverse exploratory adventures of contemporary man and, above all, the sacred sciences, St Thomas, St Bonaventure, patrology (all of it!) – not to speak just now of the Bible – none of them that is not welcomed and made vital by this great mind.[1]

Von Balthasar's range of interests, literary, cultural, philosophical as well as theological, is vast – as the long indexes to each of the volumes of his trilogy bear witness. Yet, as we have seen from our brief survey of his life, there were a series of significant relationships which occurred at crucial times, each of which were to exercise a particular influence upon his theological development. So it may be useful at this point to look once more at these important encounters and explore what issues they raised for von Balthasar, to see if these same issues are not ones which will emerge in the pages of his great trilogy. And helpfully, von Balthasar himself offered some pointers as to where we might start to look.

2.1 HENRI DE LUBAC AND HIS REDISCOVERY
OF THE FATHERS

In 1965, shortly before the completion of his *Theological Aesthetics*, the first part of his trilogy, von Balthasar offered his own reflections on those key people who had influenced his writings in an article entitled 'In Retrospect'.[2] As he looked back to the early days of his Jesuit training, what mattered to him and his contemporaries, he wrote, was to break down the bastions of anxiety by which the Church sought to protect herself *from* the world in order to free and open the Church to the saving mission of God in Christ *for* the world. And within the Order, there was one man in particular who pointed a way forward. 'This pathos rallied us young theologians . . . around our older friend and master Henri de Lubac, whose *Catholicisme* I soon translated into German' (Riches 1986: 195).

We have already noted how it was this meeting and friendship with de Lubac which helped von Balthasar to survive what he regarded as the most dreary part of his Jesuit training at Fourvière, his struggles with what he elsewhere described as 'dry as sawdust Thomism'. De Lubac's role was significant, not just to clarify what was missing in his formal studies, but also to point the way forward to where such a fresh perspective might be found. 'In Lyons during my theological studies, it was the encounter with Henri de Lubac that decided the direction of my studies', von Balthasar wrote, before adding somewhat deprecatingly, 'Because exegesis was weak, the Fathers easily won the upper hand'. Following the lead offered by de Lubac, it was von Balthasar's rediscovery of the Fathers which opened his eyes to a world which still bore the divine image and remained hopeful of being transformed by the glory of God. 'For patristics meant to us a Christendom which still carried its thoughts into the limitless space of the nations and still trusted in the world's salvation.' (Riches 1986: 195) And it was this inspiration which led von Balthasar to plan his first theological works, a trilogy based on the writings of Origen, Gregory of Nyssa and Maximus the Confessor.

The significance of this rediscovery of the Fathers for von Balthasar's theology will become evident also in the *Trilogy*, not least in Volume II of his *Aesthetics* in which, as we shall see, there are substantial sections engaging with Irenaeus, Augustine and Denys the Pseudo-Areopagite. Moreover, it is not just von Balthasar's word that we need take on the subject; the importance of this patristic influence has also been picked up in a number of recent books, not least by the American scholar Kevin Mongrain who gives his study, *The Systematic Thought of*

Hans Urs von Balthasar, the sub-title *An Irenaean Retrieval.* Mongrain argues that the foundational theme which runs through all of von Balthasar's work is 'Irenaeus' paradoxical and doxological theology of the mutual glorification of God and creation' (Mongrain 2002: 28), a theme summed up in Irenaeus' celebrated doctrine of 'recapitulation', the idea that in Christ God was involved not just in redeeming but in restoring and recreating his world afresh.

However a closer reading of Mongrain reveals that within this account the influence of de Lubac is still evident. For it is not just Irenaeus *tout simple*, bur rather Irenaeus as interpreted by Lubac who is the decisive influence on von Balthasar. 'Irenaeus, read through de Lubac's lens, therefore became von Balthasar's primary critical resource from the patristic archive for reforming contemporary Catholic theology and challenging various modern intellectual movements in theology, culture and politics' (Mongrain 2002: 16). For reasons which will become clear later, this may overstate things in terms of de Lubac's overarching importance; but that he was a significant influence is not to be doubted. Hence von Balthasar's own acknowledgment 'In Retrospect', 'From de Lubac we gained an understanding of the Greek Fathers, the philosophical mysticism of Asia, and the phenomenon of modern atheism; to him my patristic studies owe their initial spark' (Riches 1986: 195).

2.2 ERICH PRZYWARA AND THE ANALOGY OF BEING

However, it was not only de Lubac whom von Balthasar acknowledged as a key influence. In the same article he refers to another Jesuit colleague whom we have already met, namely Erich Przywara. To von Balthasar, Przywara was 'an unforgettable guide and master', one in whom he had never since encountered 'such a combination of depth and fullness of analytic clarity and all-embracing synoptic vision'. He then went on to assert that 'none of my own books should hide what it owes to him' (Riches 1986: 219). However, to understand what it was that von Balthasar learnt from Przywara and how this might be reflected in his own writings, we need first to take a step back in time to evaluate what Przywara's decisive contribution was.

We have already noted that von Balthasar first came across Przywara while doing his Jesuit training at Pullach and that he then went to stay with him for a further two years while working on the journal *Stimmen der Zeit*. What particularly struck von Balthasar about Przywara, and which contrasted with so much of his training as a Jesuit, was his sense of a Catholic faith which sought not to separate and withdraw from the world but rather to engage and interact with it. This was a major theme of Przywara since his early work *Gottgeheimnis der Welt* (or *The Mystery of God in the World*) published in 1923. Indeed, by the time that von Balthasar met him Przywara had become known as one of the leading spokesman able to articulate a Catholic viewpoint and philosophy in dialogue both with Protestant thought and also the various contemporary developments in culture and philosophy of inter-war Europe.

It was this commitment to engage with the contemporary world which von Balthasar found himself sharing as he wrote articles for *Stimmen der Zeit*. Indeed it was a similar approach that he was to adopt on his return to Switzerland as war threatened, with the series of small volumes for the Klosterberg edition, seeking to preserve the best of European culture for the Catholic community facing the onslaught of Nazism. But it was not just a general perspective which von Balthasar learnt from Przywara; nor just that sense of personal indebtedness which led him later to publish a collected edition of Przywara's work through his own publishing house, or to try and secure safe passage to Switzerland and pastoral care for Przywara after his breakdown in 1947. There was also a specific approach to the relationship between theology and philosophy which was focused on Przywara's development of the concept of the *analogia entis* or the 'analogy of being'.

Analogical thinking, the notion that there can be a relationship between two entities allowing for some similarity and equivalence without insisting on either a total identity or a total distinction, had been a part of metaphysical discourse since the days of Greek philosophy. There is also a sense in which it had been implicit in Christian theology since the time of the Chalcedonian definitions of christology, since the doctrine of the two natures in Christ assumed an analogical understanding of nature in terms of a relationship between the human and divine natures in Christ. What Przywara sought to do was to develop this concept of analogy in such a way that it provided the key to understanding not just the classical doctrines of theology, but the nature of God's engagement and the challenge of human existence in the contemporary world.

In doing this Przywara was to develop two concepts from Catholic tradition. The first was Aquinas' notion of the real distinction between God's 'essence' and his 'existence' (i.e. that God's way of being is different from that of all other creatures, in that they are dependent upon God for their existence and so are 'contingent' while God is not dependent upon anyone so that God's being and existence are 'consistent' in God's self). The second was the teaching of the Fourth Lateran Council on analogy (i.e. that 'between the Creator and the creature however great the similarity, even greater is the dissimilarity to be noted') in order to develop the concept of analogy in a way which was both comprehensive and contemporary. For Przywara, these came together in the *analogia entis* or 'analogy of being' and it was only this concept which could hold together the tension between God's transcendence (God over us) and God's immanence (God in us).

It was this tension, or 'polarity', which was characteristic of human existence as humanity sought to understand itself in relationship with God (and it was no coincidence that Przywara's major work was later translated and subtitled as *Polarity: A German Catholic's Interpretation of Religion*). In another work in 1926, *Weg zu Gott*, he wrote, '*The* primordial metaphysical fact is the tension of the analogy of "being" or expressed differently, the tension between "God in us" and "God over us," or once more, the tension between the self-reality and self-spontaneity of the creature and the universal and total reality and spontaneity of God . . . ' (Quoted in Oakes 1994: 33). And for Przywara, the crucial thing was the way that this tension was transformed and overcome by Jesus Christ, the one who, as fully man and fully God, comes as the unique personification of the analogy of being.

For our purposes the key thing to note from this is not just that this concept was known and reviewed by von Balthasar, who was to write an introduction to Przywara's theology as well as publishing his works, but that the 'analogy of being' was also to play a key structural role in the composition of his own theological trilogy, as we shall explore later. But in order to understand just how significant a concept this was to become for him, we need also to see how Przywara's work had an impact not just on von Balthasar but also on another of his major influences, namely the great Reformed theologian Karl Barth.

2.3 KARL BARTH, CHRISTOCENTRISM AND THE ANALOGY OF FAITH

We have already noted the significance of von Balthasar's encounter with Karl Barth in Basel in terms of his career and development. This meeting came at a crucial time for both of them. For Barth it came after not just his ejection from his chair at Bonn but also his conscious decision to separate himself from the so-called 'dialectical theology' movement of which he had been one of the principal protagonists and it coincided with his move towards a more constructive and systematic theology begun in the first volumes of his *Church Dogmatics*. For the younger von Balthasar, having chosen to return to Switzerland after completing his training, there had emerged the strong sense that Catholicism needed to re-engage with all the riches of her tradition if she was to resist the growing threat of fascism and totalitarianism.

So at this time of encounter both of them had the sense of something being wrong with their respective traditions which needed to be put right. For Barth it was the need for a constructive and christocentric theology to replace both the liberal Protestantism which he had already rejected and the dialectical theology he had come to regard as a dead end. Moreover in Barth's writings, von Balthasar found a fresh engagement with two of the same things which he had discovered in the Fathers, but not in his Jesuit training. The first was a fierce concentration upon God's self-revelation in Jesus Christ as the only place for theology to begin; and the second was a deep sense of joy and wonder in encountering that revelation, a real and redeeming awareness of the beauty of God.

Out of their different, but mutually supportive and encouraging experiences there developed between these two theologians a deep ecumenical friendship, in which both came to see how they were each engaging with the riches of their different traditions at a profound level. It was a relationship nurtured by a shared love of music, particularly the music of Mozart, in which both theologians heard something of the divine joy and wonder at play. And out of this friendship, and the many seminars and meetings they attended, came von Balthasar's seminal study, *The Theology of Karl Barth.*

This study was a hugely important book for three reasons. In the first place, it was the first major study of Barth's theology from an explicitly Catholic perspective, so that in addition to interpreting Barth's work von Balthasar was also looking to make a response as a Catholic theologian to some of the challenges Barth had laid down from his own Reformed tradition. Secondly, it was because von Balthasar saw in Barth's move, away from dialectical theology to a more constructive dogmatic theology based on analogy, a change in theological method. And thirdly, this was crucial, because von Balthasar's way of interpreting this, in terms of a 'conversion' from dialectic to analogy, meant that he was taking up a debate which had already begun between Barth and his former mentor Erich Przywara.

Von Balthasar proposed, picking up on something which Barth himself had acknowledged, that this change in theological approach had its origins in a short but hugely significant study Barth had made of Anselm, *Fides Quaerens Intellectum*, published in 1930. In this study, and in reflection on how the name of God as 'that than which nothing greater can be thought' was revealed to Anselm, Barth came to a clearer understanding of the relationship between faith and reason, and how theology could speak properly and objectively about God's revelation in Christ. This method was to bear fruit in the later volumes of the *Church Dogmatics*, in particular those which saw Barth's majestic reinterpretation of the doctrine of Election. For it was Barth's christological reformulation of this doctrine, showing how Christ served as both subject and object of election, both gracious God and the man chosen for damnation and salvation, which provided the basis for the relationship between creation and covenant, and thus the methodological key to interpret the whole story of salvation.

What von Balthasar was suggesting was that this development could best be seen in terms of a move away from dialectical to analogical thinking. Moreover, in doing this he was picking up on that major theme previously identified by his friend and colleague Erich Przywara, namely the *analogia entis* or 'analogy of being'. We have already noted how Przywara had come to

view this as the key to a proper Catholic understanding of life
and faith. But for Barth, who had himself met up with Przywara
while at the University of Münster in the 1920's, it was a concept
which remained deeply flawed. However impressive Przywara's
presentation of the concept of analogy might be, it was nevertheless a concept drawn not from God's revelation in scripture
but from human reasoning and was thus symptomatic of the
way in which the Catholic Church had sought to shape the revelation of God from within a philosophical framework which
instead depended upon the assertion of human rationality. For
this reason alone it could not be the basis of a Christ-centred
theology. (Indeed in an early volume of his *Dogmatics*, Barth
famously called the *analogia entis* 'the invention of the anti-
Christ' and went on to offer instead the *analogia fidei* or 'analogy
of faith', in which the nature of any similarity in relationship
between human and divine being was to be interpreted and
understood only in light of the revelation of God and from the
perspective of faith in Christ.)

More recently, and particularly since the publication of Bruce
McCormack's major study of Barth's theological development,[3]
there has been some questioning of the accuracy of von
Balthasar's interpretation of Barth in terms of a move from dialectic to analogy. There is debate about how well such a thesis
actually fits with the historical development of Barth's writings
as well as discussion about far the changes and developments in
Barth's theology run alongside deeper consistencies in this
thought. But what is important for our study is not so much what
took place in terms of Barth's development, but the importance
of what von Balthasar discovered and took seriously for his own
theology, particularly in light of what he clearly saw as Barth's
challenge to the Catholic tradition in which he had grown up.

For while he recognized and rejoiced in Barth's rediscovery of
the beauty of God's revelation in Christ, and admired the way in
which Barth took this christological focus and used it as the
central point of his mature theology, he was also convinced that
Barth had misunderstood his colleague and mentor Przywara.
He was convinced that Przywara's understanding of the analogy
of being, christologically reinterpreted, actually served to
address some of the weaknesses which von Balthasar had found
in his study of Barth, not least the charge of what he called

christological 'constriction', the idea that Barth had so drawn things together in Christ that there was little room left for an appropriate human response and engagement, that in all the focus upon God's revelation in Christ there was insufficient space allowed for that participation in the divine act of salvation which would lead to the transformation of the life of the believer.

I have elsewhere described this meeting between the two theologians 'a critical engagement' (Wigley 2007), and I believe this to be an accurate description in both senses of the word 'critical', especially for von Balthasar. It was critical both in terms of what von Balthasar discovered positively in Barth and which served to shape his own theological development; and also negatively, in that at the same time it also challenged and provoked him into offering an alternative response to some of the issues which Barth had raised. Barth was not the only influence at work in his great trilogy; but that Barth played a crucial role seems to me not in doubt. In light of this encounter it can come as no surprise that von Balthasar's own trilogy is based round the fundamentals of being, takes analogy as a key concept, and begins with an Aesthetics which focuses on the glory of God. However, there remains one other lifelong influence on von Balthasar whom we have already met but need also to explore further now.

2.4 ADRIENNE VON SPEYR AND THE ROLE OF RELIGIOUS EXPERIENCE

We have already observed the profound influence which Adrienne von Speyr was to have on von Balthasar's life and faith, not least in his decision to leave the Society of Jesus and with her to set up the Community of St John. In a little book which von Balthasar wrote setting out the importance of her life and writings, *First Glance at Adrienne von Speyr*,[4] he maintained that, 'I not only made some of the most difficult decisions of my life – including my leaving the Jesuit Order – following her advice, but I also strove to bring my way of looking at Christian revelation into conformity with hers'. In his mind it was also clear that she was to have an equally important influence on his work and writings, going on to write that, 'On the whole I received far more from her, theologically, than she from me, though, of course, the exact proportion can never be calculated' (*FG*: 13).

However, this is not an opinion which everyone would share. We have already noted how controversial a figure Adrienne proved to be, both for von Balthasar's superiors and for his wider reception of his work by the Catholic authorities. Some of the same questions remain concerning the influence which she had on his writings. There is no doubt of von Balthasar's commitment to her cause, as witnessed by his transcription of so many volumes of her visions and mystical commentaries particularly on the Johannine writings. It is more of a question as to how far these writings and their shared experiences served to influence von Balthasar's own maturing theology. Given the uncertainty about Adrienne and the reception of their joint project among Vatican circles right up till the end of von Balthasar's life, this is a subject which remains a matter of some debate.

It is clear that von Balthasar himself seeks to acknowledge her throughout the trilogy and her influence is most clearly seen in two areas. The first is to do with the role of religious experience itself. Von Balthasar was himself trained in the Ignatian order of spirituality and became a noted leader of retreats during which the emphasis was on developing the spiritual senses and imagination so as to experience the truth of the Gospel story in a vivid and life-transforming way. Reading his trilogy, and in particular those volumes of the *Theological Aesthetics* which give an account of the development of Christian spirituality, it becomes clear that one of the things von Balthasar is seeking to do is to reclaim the role of religious experience as part of mainstream Christian discipleship, and not as something restricted to a few saints and mystics. This was something he would claim as one of Adrienne's major achievements. 'Adrienne von Speyr has brought mysticism back from the clandestine existence into which, increasingly misunderstood, indeed scorned, it had been exiled and silenced by official theology and proclamation, and returned it to the centre of salvation history' (*FG*: 89). In this way he might be seen to be reclaiming for Catholic orthodoxy those mystical experiences of Adrienne which were questioned during her lifetime.

The second is to do with von Balthasar's reading of the Bible and in particular his interpretation of aspects of the Easter story as read through the Gospel narratives. There are times in his trilogy when von Balthasar's exposition appears to be heavily influenced by some of Adrienne's visions and commentaries. This is particular the case in his treatment of what has become known as Holy Saturday, the day when Christ descends to the depths of Hell in order to cleanse it and sanctify it in the power of the resurrection. The reality of Christ's abandonment to suffering and death while still being held in the knowledge and love of God is given extraordinary power by the emotional depth and profundity of Adrienne's experiences and it is here that her influence on his writings perhaps reaches its peak, in her account of the 'descent into hell'. It is this which von Balthasar regarded as 'the greatest theological gift she received from God and left to the Church' (*FG*: 64), and it is this which would influence his own account of the saving activity of God in his *Dramatics* (as well as in some of his other writings, for example his widely influential *Mysterium Paschale*, the Mystery of Easter).

However, while the impact of Adrienne von Speyr is evident in these aspects of his writings, it is less clear that her influence has served to shape the highly distinctive structure of his trilogy taken as a whole. So for all that von Balthasar himself claimed that, for example, 'the basic perspective of *Herrlichkeit* would never have existed' without her encouragement (*FG*: 13), it is more likely that those other influences which we have already identified in terms of Henri de Lubac, Erich Przywara and Karl Barth may have had more of an impact in terms of its overall structure. But in order for us properly to assess this, we need to turn to the trilogy itself and to see how von Balthasar's great programmatic work unfolds.

2.5 VON BALTHASAR'S USE OF SOURCES

Before doing this however, there is one further aspect of von Balthasar's work which we would do well to note. We have already made reference to his friend Henri de Lubac's assessment of his being 'perhaps the most cultivated of our time'. This is quite evident to any reader in the way von Balthasar approaches the vast arena of his theological project. It means that in the course of engaging with any particular theme, it will not be unusual to discover him referring to a wide range of sources which may include Greek philosophy, the writings of the early Church Fathers (not just the principal figures such as Augustine but also lesser known ones such as Denys the Pseudo-Areopagite and Maximus the Confessor), Anselm and Aquinas, the medieval scholastics and later Reformers, right the way through to the German idealists and his own theological debating partners in the twentieth century.

Moreover, von Balthasar does not merely refer to them, but in many instances offers extended quotations and summaries from their work, a reflection, no doubt, of the fact that he himself has already published detailed studies of their work on other occasions. Apart from reminding any reviewer of the daunting range of his literary and theological output, this can make von Balthasar's work difficult to summarize in short space and can, on occasions, make his narrative thread difficult to follow, as his writing seems to range effortlessly over centuries of thought and debate.

However, it is also characteristic of von Balthasar that throughout his theological works, and especially in his trilogy, he seeks to allow space for his theological partners to speak for themselves before putting his own distinctive cast and interpretation on the result. It seems to me that, despite the challenge of covering so vast a topic as his trilogy in so short a space, his is not a bad approach to follow. Accordingly in the chapters which follow, I will seek wherever possible to allow von Balthasar to speak for himself, to allow him his own choice of words to illustrate the points he is making, while at the same time offering summaries of my own as to the structure of his work and the direction his theological trilogy is taking us.

CHAPTER 3

THE GLORY OF THE LORD: A THEOLOGICAL AESTHETICS

INTRODUCTION

The Glory of the Lord is the first part of von Balthasar's great trilogy. It comprises some seven volumes running to three and a half thousand pages and is a major work of theology in its own right. It also has a very distinctive shape and structure, which reflects some of the influences that we have already noted, but which is worth setting out in outline before addressing each of the volumes in turn.

In *The Glory of the Lord* von Balthasar consciously models his work on the beautiful, as the first of the transcendentals of being. In doing this he is picking up on that recovery of the divine glory which is part of what he had discovered in Karl Barth. However, he is doing this within a framework in which he will insist on the crucial importance of analogy, and especially the analogy of being, which has been part of the debate between Barth and Przywara and which he has taken on further. Within the respective volumes we will also find extensive reference to the role of the Church Fathers, including complete sections on Irenaeus, Augustine and Denys the Pseudo-Areopagite, as well as a thorough reassessment of the role of religious experience as part of mainstream Christian life and faith. These in turn reflect the influence of Henri de Lubac and Adrienne von Speyr as we have previously noted.

What gives *The Glory of the Lord* its particular shape is two things: the first is that von Balthasar is seeking to recover for Christian theology a proper aesthetic and appreciation of the divine beauty which he believes has been lost; and the second is that he regards this loss of aesthetic vision to have its origins in the disintegration of a unified concept of being in the years after

Thomas Aquinas (following the development of the scholastic method and the rise of the natural sciences). What this means for his *Aesthetics* is that it will be a conscious attempt to redress something which has gone wrong: first identifying the problem, then giving accounts of other attempts to address it, before then offering his own and very distinctive solution, including an aesthetic reading of the Bible in terms of giving glory to God.

This very distinctive structure has been characterized by the American scholar Edward Oakes as 'the archaeology of alienated beauty', in which von Balthasar addresses the question 'whence came this silent cataclysm that hurled some of the Church's greatest artists, writers and apologists out into the most distant orbits of her gravitational field?' *The Glory of the Lord* represents von Balthasar's own distinctive answer which Oakes summarizes as follows, 'If *Clerical* and *Lay Styles* may be said to display the symptomatics of this alienation, the next two volumes *Metaphysics in Antiquity* and *Modernity* may be called its diagnostics, while the last two volumes *Old* and *New Covenant* attempt to offer the cure – the "prognostics" we might say' (Oakes 1994: 176). This is brought home in the original German edition in which the books on *Styles*, *Metaphysics* and the *Covenant* are published as parts one and two of the same volume. (We should also note that that an additional final volume, planned in terms of an ecumenical theology by way of Byzantium – Rome – Wittenberg, was never written, perhaps because so much of the ecumenical material had already been included elsewhere.)

However, having drawn attention to the particular structure and shape of this work, it is now time to address the first volume in his *Aesthetics*, namely *Seeing the Form*.

3.1 *SEEING THE FORM*

'Beauty is the word that shall be our first' (*GL1*: 18). This may seem an odd place for a theologian to begin, as von Balthasar himself recognizes. 'Beauty is the last thing which the thinking intellect dares to approach, since only it dances as an uncontained splendour around the double constellation of the true and the good and their inseparable relation to one another.' But that only serves to render its role more important; for in a world without beauty even the good and the true are threatened with incomprehension.

> In a world without beauty – even if people cannot dispense with the word and constantly have it on the tip of their tongues in order to abuse it – in a world which is perhaps not wholly without beauty, but which can no longer see it or reckon with it: in such a world the good also loses its attractiveness, the self-evidence of why it must be carried out. (*GL1*: 19)

However, to engage with the beautiful means also to engage with form. 'Those words which attempt to convey the beautiful gravitate, first of all, toward the mystery of form (*Gestalt*) or of figure (*Gebilde*)' (*GL1*: 19). Von Balthasar's conviction is that there can be no beauty without form just as there can be no person without a life-form. 'What is a person without a life-form, that is to say without a form which he has chosen for his life, a form into which and through which to pour out his life, so that his life becomes the soul of the form and the form becomes the expression of his soul?' (*GL1*: 24).

From this it follows that 'to be a Christian is precisely a form. How could it be otherwise since being a Christian is a grace, a possibility of existence opened up by God's act of justification, by the God-Man's act of redemption?' The Christian finds fulfilment and realises his mission 'only if he truly *becomes* this form which has been willed and instituted by Christ' (*GL1*: 28). This in turn points to what must be the starting point for any Christian aesthetic or theology: 'the form of divine revelation in salvation-history, leading to Christ and deriving from him' as 'God's Incarnation perfects the whole ontology and aesthetics of created being' (*GL1*: 29). This is a form which unites both salvation-history and the created cosmos and which is 'constituted by the Old and New Testaments together' (*GL1*: 30). Moreover, mindful of what he terms the principle of the 'indissolubility of form', von Balthasar warns against trying to find a deeper meaning by breaking up and delving behind the existing form. 'For we can be sure of one thing: we can never again recapture the living totality of form once it has been dissected and sawn into pieces, no matter how informative the conclusions this anatomy may bring to light' (*GL1*: 31).

Having established the central importance of form, von Balthasar goes on to address the obvious question that follows; how far can the form of beauty in the natural world be subject to the same principles as the divine beauty? This raises the issue of analogy, an issue which von Balthasar recognizes has its dangers but is nevertheless essential to the task; for 'if God's will to give form really aims at man as God truly wants to shape him . . . then it appears impossible to deny that there exists an analogy between God's work of formation and the shaping forces of nature and of man as they generate and give birth' (*GL1*: 36).

Von Balthasar then offers a brief survey of how far the Church Fathers managed to address this issue, recognizing that 'even such a historical reminder cannot go beyond a theoretical and practical call to the constant vigilance required to keep the transcendental beauty of revelation from slipping into equality with an inner-worldly natural beauty' (*GL1*: 41). This is followed by a short summary of how the Bible treats the issue of 'the beauty of revelation', noting its different forms, the significant passages which are in poetry rather than prose, and the importance of the Wisdom tradition, in which 'there emerges spontaneously an unmistakeable aesthetic element' (*GL1*: 42). His conclusion is that to try and excise such elements from Scripture 'would mean abandoning the historical setting of the Biblical revelation' leaving it with only 'a certain moralism which was non-historical and therefore, however existential, ultimately ineffective' (*GL1*: 45).

However, this is precisely what von Balthasar believes to have happened with the Protestant Reformation. Luther's theology of the Cross, Hegel's dialectical theology and Kierkegaard's rejection of the aesthetics of liberal protestant theology as influenced by Schleiermacher lead to what von Balthasar describes as the '"either/or" of this crossroads': 'on the one hand, the radical elimination of aesthetics from theology, and on the other, a paradoxical "aestheticization" which would again logically bring about a new and sweeping iconoclastic controversy' (*GL1*: 48) Or perhaps, as von Balthasar later suggests when writing of Bultmann's theology, 'this is a gravity which, alas, is full of anguish because of its total lack of imagery and form: a real dead-end for Protestantism' (*GL1*: 52).

It is at this point that von Balthasar turns to one of the key influences whom we have already identified. The loss of beauty and transcendence in theology was something which von Balthasar knew to his own cost. It had been all too true of his own experience of theological training by the Jesuits at Four-vière. However, in this struggle, he was to find that he was not alone; for in his meeting with Karl Barth, he had come to recognize that that there was another theologian who was equally keen to restore the importance of beauty as a theological concept. This was not simply the matter of Barth's adopting a particular theological style or way of writing. Rather it came from his object-ive engagement with the proper object of theology, namely God in his revelation, combined with a passionate enthusiasm, as he is drawn into the beauty and joy of his subject matter. 'Barth focuses on the Word, fully and exclusively, that its full splendour might radiate out to the reader. Who but Barth has gazed so breathlessly and tirelessly on his subject, watching it develop and blossom in all its power before his eyes?' And in turn it meant that, 'For Barth, the religious sphere is aesthetical because it is religious, because it is in itself the most authentic' (*KB*: 26).

In light of this recognition, perhaps we should not be surprised to find that at this point in his introduction, von Balthasar turns to acknowledge 'the great service rendered to theology by Karl Barth of having recognized the imminent danger of shipwreck and of having, unaided, put the helm hard over'. Von Balthasar understands this in terms of Barth's overcoming the 'either/or' between Hegel and Kierkegaard, recognizing the need (with Hegel) for an objectively formed dogmatics but also (with Kierkegaard) for this to have as its content the personal faith relationship, mediated through Jesus Christ. In turn his insistence upon the 'real form' of God's revelation in Christ, leads him 'at the conclusion of his treatment of the doctrine of the divine perfections, to restore to God the attribute of "beauty" for the first time in the history of Protestant theology' (*GL1*: 53). However, just as important for von Balthasar is the fact that 'Barth arrives at the content of "beauty" in a purely theological manner, namely, by contemplating the data of Scripture, especially God's "glory," for whose interpretation " beauty" appears to him indispensable as "auxiliary concept"' (*GL1*: 53).

Von Balthasar demonstrates this with reference to Barth's exposition of 'The Eternity and Glory of God' in Volume II.1 of the *Church Dogmatics*. God is 'beautiful in a manner proper to him and to him alone' as 'the one who arouses *pleasure* (*Wohlgefallen*), creates *desire* (*Begehren*) for himself, and rewards with *delight* (*Genuss*) . . . the one who as God is both *lovely* and *love-worthy*'. This means that both the concept of beauty must be taken seriously ('Much too much would have to be deleted . . . which in the Bible is clearly and loudly proclaimed, if we were to attempt to deny the legitimacy of the concept of beauty . . .') and so also 'the question of form' ('if revelation's quality of beaming forth joy is not adequately appreciated, where exactly then – so important is this question of form! – would be the gladness of the Glad Tidings?') (*GL1*: 53–5).

For von Balthasar, form can not be separated from content, and he notes how Barth goes on to follow Anselm in calling theology the 'most beautiful of all the sciences', because of the beauty of its contents, namely its contemplation of God's being in himself, in the relations of the Trinity, and in the Incarnation of the eternal Son. Moreover, it is through contemplation of the Incarnation that the particular form of God's beauty is perceived and this carries through to contemplation of the cross; 'If we seek Christ's beauty in a glory which is not that of the Crucified, we are doomed to seek in vain'. 'In this self-revelation, God's beauty embraces death as well as life, fear as well as joy, what we call "ugly" as well as what we call "beautiful"' (*GL1*: 55–6).

Here von Balthasar believes that Barth has made a significant contribution to theology. In contrast to the main thrust of Protestant theology, which following Luther has largely denied the role of aesthetics, Barth has recovered the concept of beauty in terms of the glory of God. He has rediscovered those roots which underlie the reformers and go back deeper to the patristic period, to the works of Augustine and Pseudo-Denys. But despite this achievement, von Balthasar claims that he has not really altered the trend of Protestant theology as a whole, which 'continues in dutiful subservience to Bultmann's dualism of criticism, on the one hand, and existential, imageless inwardness on the other. Contemporary Protestant theology nowhere deals with the beautiful as a theological category' (*GL1*: 56).

Moreover, there is a question in von Balthasar's mind as to whether this is simply because Barth's approach has not been heeded – or whether instead his approach has not gone far enough. Having demonstrated the inadequacy of a theology denuded of aesthetics, and thereby deprived of appreciation of the loveliness of God, that quality which draws humanity close and makes the gospel good news, von Balthasar follows up with an overview of the different ways in which theologians, both Protestant and Catholic, have tried largely without success to reintroduce the concept of beauty and the role of aesthetics. These attempts have been complicated by the development of secular ideals of beauty, particularly in response to the Idealist and Romantic movements in European thought, which have resulted in attempts at an aesthetic theology rather than a properly grounded theological aesthetic.

However, the challenge which von Balthasar has posed remains.

> Should we go the way of Karl Barth, who rediscovers the inner beauty of theology and revelation itself? Or (and this is perhaps implicitly included in Barth's position), may it not be that we have a real and inescapable obligation to probe the possibility of there being a genuine relationship between theological beauty and the beauty of the world . . . ? (*GL1*: 80)

Von Balthasar's query is about whether in focusing so strictly on the God's beauty in revelation, Barth has failed to allow sufficiently for the possibility for an ontological relationship between the Creator and his creation. And his response to this challenge is set out in summary form at the end of his introduction under the heading 'The Task and the Structure of a Theological Aesthetics' (*GL1*: 117–27). It is to build on the exploration of aesthetics found in classical antiquity, but to ground it thoroughly in the form of God's revelation in Jesus Christ and to ally to his exposition something of the passionate yearning which can be found in Pseudo-Denys and other Christian writings.

Von Balthasar starts with two aspects which have been found in every exploration of beauty, and which since Aquinas have been termed *species* (or *forma*) and *lumen* (or *splendor*) – that is 'form' (*Gestalt*) and 'splendour' (*Glanz*). The perception of beauty consists both of an appreciation of the form or shape in which it appears, and of the extent to which that form points towards a deeper reality, the hidden depths which subsist below the object which is perceived. Thus, 'The appearance of the form, as revelation of the depths, is an indissoluble union of two things. It is the real presence of the depths, of the whole of reality, *and* it is a real pointing beyond itself to these depths' (*GL1*: 118). Different periods of intellectual history have appreciated one aspect more than the other; the classical period concentrating more on the form and the Romantic movement more on the hidden depths beneath. However, the truth is that both of them belong together and are inseparable in any perception of beauty.

However, because the perception of beauty involves both the form in which it appears and the hidden depths to which it points, there is also a sense in which beauty is not just in the eye of the beholder, but includes also that movement by which the beholder is drawn into, indeed 'enraptured' by, the splendour and glory of being itself (*GL1*: 119). This means that to offer a theory of perception, which for von Balthasar is an encounter with being itself, there can be no simple or univocal application of philosophical categories used to describe or explain the existence of earthly entities (and here von Balthasar is understanding of those who from a Protestant perspective have been critical of too close an appropriation of pre-Christian Greek philosophy). Instead, what is required is an analogical approach, as is suggested by the form of God's revelation in the world, in its creation, reconciliation and redemption.

Given the centrality of the Incarnation to his thought, perhaps it is not surprising that von Balthasar finds a key to illustrate what is happening in the Christmas Preface. '*Quia per incarnati Verbi mysterium nova mentis nostrae oculis lux tuae claritatis infulsit: ut dum visibiliter Deum cognoscimus, per hunc in invisibilium amorem rapiamur.*' (Because through the mystery of the incarnate Word the new light of your brightness has shone onto the eyes of our mind; that knowing God visibly, we might be snatched up by this into the love of invisible things (*GL1*:119–20).) This prayer emphasizes how it is by the perception of what we do see that we are drawn into the mystery of that which we cannot see. But it also shows how this is not initiated simply by the act of perception, but that it is the beauty of God's revelation which so enraptures the beholder that we are drawn into the mystery of God's presence.

It also focuses on the role of desire in seeking God's presence and beauty, that *eros* which von Balthasar finds in the writings of Pseudo-Denys (who will be one of the theologians to be examined later in Volume II) and in whom he finds a resonance with that enthusiasm and longing for the presence of God found throughout the Bible. He is aware of the need to be careful in the use of such classical sources, 'Because God actually effects that which he reveals in the sign, and because in God's order of salvation Plato's idealistic *imago*-metaphysics and Aristotle's realistic *causa-et-finis* metaphysics actually come together on a higher plane, we can never approach Christian *eros* and Christian beauty from a merely Platonic tradition and expect to interpret them adequately'. Nevertheless, von Balthasar maintains, 'All divine revelation is impregnated with a sense of "enthusiasm" (in the theological sense). Nothing be done for the person who can not detect such an element in the Prophets and the "teachers of wisdom", in Paul and John, to mention only these' (*GL1*: 123).

This enthusiasm, this longing for the beauty and presence of God, is not an idealistic one based on false illusions and misconceptions, the kind of false enthusiasm which von Balthasar finds condemned in the New Testament epistles; rather it is 'an enthusiasm which derives from and is appropriate to actual, realistic Being'. This means in turn, that it is not merely content with the glory of worldly beauty, but can also interpret, indeed transfigure those aspects which a worldly aesthetic regard as ugly. For, 'As Karl Barth has rightly seen, this law extends to the inclusion in Christian beauty of even the Cross and everything else which a worldly aesthetics (even of a realistic kind) discards as no longer bearable' (*GL1*: 123–4).

The conclusions which von Balthasar draws from this for his *Theological Aesthetics* are as follows. In the first place, it must be resolutely christological; for 'just as we can never attain to the living God in any way except through his Son become man, but in this Son we can really attain to God in himself, so too, we ought never to speak of God's beauty without reference to the form and manner of his appearing which he exhibits in salvation-history' (*GL1*: 124). But this is not to be done in such a way that the perception of God's beauty is simply *equated* with the manner of his appearing. There is a need both to perceive the form and to be drawn in to those hidden depths which lie beneath the form. As the words of the Christmas preface suggest, this requires in turn both a *theologia positiva* which examines the form and content of revelation and a *theologia negativa* which recognizes the mystery of those things which we cannot see.

Finally, this means that a theological aesthetics must be developed in two stages. In the first place there is required a 'theory of vision', that is a 'theory about the perception of the form of God's self-revelation' (which von Balthasar categorizes as 'fundamental theology'). But alongside this there is also needed a 'theory of rapture', that is a 'theory about the incarnation of God's glory and the consequent elevation of man to participate in that glory' (which he categorizes as 'dogmatic theology') (*GL1*: 125). But these cannot be developed separately or independently of each other, since von Balthasar maintains that there are no 'bare facts' which can be apprehended or interpreted outside of the realm of grace. 'For the object with which we are concerned is man's participation in God which, from God's perspective, is actualized as "revelation" (culminating in Christ's Godmanhood) and which, from man's perspective, is actualized as "faith" (culminating in participation in Christ's Godmanhood)' (*GL1*: 125).

Von Balthasar recognizes that such a starting point for his *Aesthetics* has huge methodological implications. 'For it would follow that fundamental theology and dogmatic theology – the theory of vision and the theory of rapture – are, in the last analysis, inseparable' (*GL1*: 126). Admittedly von Balthasar is here using these traditional terms of Catholic theology, 'fundamental' and 'dogmatic', in a very particular way, as the basis for a theological aesthetic which focuses on the revelation of God in Jesus Christ to show how in perceiving the form the believer is to be drawn into participating in the divine drama. But having taken this decision, the rest of the opening volume reflects the task which von Balthasar has set himself.

There are two further substantial sections. Under the heading, 'The Subjective Evidence' he expounds a theory of vision, or fundamental theology, from the perspective of human perception; then, under the heading 'The Objective Evidence' he sets out the dogmatic basis for this in terms of the revelation of God in Jesus Christ. Following on from what has already been established in the introduction, in both of these sections he will emphasize the importance of form, both in terms of its human perception, and its divine origins. However in light of the comments which he has already made about the inseparability of the two approaches, we will not be surprised to see that similar material crops up under both headings.

This much is immediately made clear from the beginning of 'The Subjective Evidence', which takes as its key concept that word which is at the heart of the two great New Testament theologies of Paul and John, namely *pistis* or faith. To recognize this is to recognize also that the distinction between subjective and objective can not be too tightly drawn. 'Such an equation presupposes that faith does not primarily mean the subjective act of faith (*fides qua*), but that faith always includes the whole substance towards which this act is directed (*fides quae*), by which the act can be understood and justified' (*GL1*: 131). There follows under the heading of 'The Light of Faith', an exploration of the relationship between *gnosis* and *pistis*, between knowing and believing, as it is found in the Bible and subsequently in the theology of the great Alexandrine theologians. The thrust of this is to insist that a properly biblical *gnosis* is not an abstract standing back from the subject matter of faith, but rather a process of participation and engagement which leads to illumination and understanding, so that von Balthasar can posit an underlying unity between seeing (knowing) and believing.

This has two consequences for von Balthasar's *Theological Aesthetics*. In the first place it means that the pursuit of knowledge and understanding is itself an inherently theological task, which suggests that the early Christian theologians were themselves building on the legacy of pre-Christian philosophers. 'Man's ultimate attitude in response to God's self-revelation can stand only in the most intimate connection with that other ultimate attitude of man which is the philosophic . . . In this context, theology clearly takes over functions which in the pre- and non-Christian world belonged to philosophy' (*GL1*: 143). It also follows that a theological approach to perception must engage with those attempts made by philosophy to attain that same knowledge and understanding. 'In other words, the formal object of theology (and, therefore, also of the act of faith) lies at the very heart of the formal object of philosophy' so that 'the self-revelation of God, who is absolute Being, can only be the fulfilment of man's entire philosophical-mythological questioning as well' (*GL1*: 145). All this points to the task which will be undertaken in the fourth and fifth volumes of *The Glory of the Lord* in which von Balthasar will examine *The Realm of Metaphysics in Antiquity* and *The Modern Age.*

But it also points to that other concept which will play much the dominant role in this examination of the subjective evidence. This is 'The Experience of Faith', for such a knowledge and understanding can come only from an experience of being drawn into and living the Christian faith. In focussing upon the role of Christian experience von Balthasar knows that he is taking a risk of being misunderstood. He anticipates this from the way in which, since the Middle Ages especially, 'experience' has been subsumed under the category of Christian mysticism and separated from the Christian mainstream. He knows it also from the way in which the Catholic Church of his own day has found it hard to assimilate and comprehend the kind of experience undergone by his colleague Adrienne von Speyr, whose insights have also been so crucial for the development of his theological trilogy.

Accordingly, it is part of von Balthasar's objective to reclaim the role of experience for the mainstream of Christian faith. He does this by examining the role of experience in the New Testament theologies of Paul and John, the way it is treated elsewhere in the Bible, and then the way it occupies such a leading role in the theology of so many of the Church Fathers (not just those leading names such as Irenaeus who will appear later in Volume II, *Clerical Styles*, but also less well-known names such as Pseudo-Macarius, Diadochus of Photice and Maximus the Confessor) before an extended treatment of how it is treated in the Middle Ages, especially by Aquinas. His conclusion is that while the treatment of this concept took its starting point from the 'unreflected unity between mystical experience and "ordinary" experience' (*GL1*: 299), it was the development of Christian mysticism as a separate and distinct vocation apart from the Christian mainstream which has resulted in its being looked upon with suspicion by the rest of the Christian community.

It is this gap which von Balthasar wants to bridge – and in this we may detect the influence also of Adrienne von Speyr. 'Precisely because mystical experience remains an experience within faith and because faith in Christ is already a genuine and objective encounter of the whole man with the Incarnate God, there exists a "radical homogeneity" between mystical experience and faith.'

But because it is so central to the Christian faith, experience is not something which can be restricted to a few experts or vocations; rather it is part and parcel of the life of the whole Church. 'The full Christian experience, however, is not an individual experience which may be isolated from all else; it is, unconditionally, an experience within the context of the Church' (*GL1*: 300). Moreover, it is this insistence upon the fundamentally *ecclesial* nature of Christian experience, which leads onto the next and crucial stage in his exposition and this is the role of *archetypal* experience in the experience of faith.

To understand the role of archetypal experience, von Balthasar maintains we must first understand 'the structure of Biblical revelation' which is made concrete in the Incarnation.

The perception of God, who is imperceivable in himself and yet has become perceivable through his free grace, is realized when God comes into the world, and, yes, *becomes world*. His allowing us to participate in his Godhead, which is above the world, precisely in this and no other way, occurs not in a second process, but in the one and only process. This is the *admirabile commercium et conubium* (the wondrous exchange and marriage). In God's condescendence lies man's exaltation. (*GL1*: 302)

Working back from this, God's revelation to the world must be considered as 'homogeneous from beginning to end', which means that God's creation is 'neither surpassed nor made superfluous for all the revelation of grace and glory'. 'The world is the stage which has been set up for the encounter of the whole God and the whole man – "stage" not as an empty space but as the sphere of collaboration of the two-sided form which unites in the encounter' (*GL1*: 303).

The consequence of this for the enactment of the drama of salvation will be worked out in the second work of his trilogy, in the *Theo-Drama*. But for now, we are concerned with form and this introduction makes it clear that 'the christological form as such is, absolutely, the form of the encounter between God and man'. This means that those experiences which are recorded in the Old Testament have a 'proleptic character', in that their structure reveals an 'anticipated Christology', notwithstanding the fact that their 'very sensoriness and their celestial symbolism is something that cannot be surpassed by the New Testament' (*GL1*: 336). (Indeed the relationship between the two Testaments will be dealt with extensively in Volume VI, *The Old Covenant.*) But it also means that the role of those who themselves encountered Christ in the course of his life and death have a particular significance for subsequent believers and the form of their encounter with Christ. Von Balthasar maintains that theirs is an archetypal experience which is demonstrated in a number of ways.

It begins with Mary. 'At the point where all roads meet which lead from the Old Testament to the New we encounter the Marian experience of God, at once so rich and so secret that it almost escapes description' (*GL1*: 338). This is followed by the experience of the Apostles, 'the founders of the Church, officially chosen and called by the Lord, whose first function will be to be eyewitnesses' (*GL1*: 343). These include not just the Twelve chosen by Jesus, who share in and bear witness to his ministry on the way to the cross, but also the apostle Paul who, as a witness '*only* to Jesus' resurrection', 'straddles the boundary between the apostolic and ecclesial era' (*GL1*: 347–8). However, the significance of these first followers of Christ lies not simply in the experience they have undergone themselves, but in the way their experience is shared with others, indeed with us. 'The archetypal experience of individual members, however, is but a privileged participation in.Christ's all-sustaining experience of God. And Christ invites the Church as a whole to participate in this experience, uniting each member of the Church directly to himself and yet, at the same time, mediating between individual members and uniting them to himself through others' (*GL1*: 350).

It is here that von Balthasar identifies the four traditions which underscore the relationship between biblical and archetypal experience and ordinary Christian experience in the Church, four traditions which, although they overlap and interpenetrate one another, nevertheless offer different modes of access.

> First there is the eyewitness of the Twelve, of which Peter is representative, and which is embodied in the Petrine tradition of the Church. Then there is the unique eyewitness of Paul, whose life-work and written legacy outstrip that of all the

others (1 Cor 15.10) and flow into the Church in a current of tradition all its own. Then there is the equally special (ocular, aural, and tactile) witness of the Beloved Disciple, who at the same time is the conscious perfector of Old Testament prophecy and who, through both these functions, lends the faith of the Church a particular colouration. Finally, at a level which is deeper and closer to the centre, there is the experience of the Lord's Mother, which wholly passes over into the Church and renders the Church fruitful. (*GL1*: 351)

It is von Balthasar's conviction that, 'All four archetypal experiences converge in the Church'. However, within this overlapping series of relationships he is also clear that the threefold archetypal experience of the Apostles remains 'permanently sustained and undergirded by the Marian experience of Christ', an experience which in common with all mothers is both 'bodily and spiritual, inseparably'. Moreover, this has consequences for the Church. 'Because Mary is bodily the Mother of the Lord, the Bride-Church must be bodily and visible, and her visible sacraments and institutions must be an occasion for the spiritual experience of Christ and of God' (*GL1*: 362–4).

From this foundation, that of sharing in the archetypal experience of both Mary and the Apostles, von Balthasar goes on to develop his position on 'the Spiritual Senses'. In this section he emphasizes the importance of both sensory and spiritual perception, echoing the model which he has found in the apostolic witness, and also re-emphasizing its proper place within the mainstream of Christian belief, rather than as the preserve of an esoteric minority. Interestingly enough, within this exposition he refers both to the application of the senses within the Ignatian tradition of spirituality, with which he would be familiar from his Jesuit training and experience of leading retreats, and also offers a sustained treatment of the biblical anthropology found in Karl Barth's *Church Dogmatics* III.2, with its emphasis upon the 'spiritual-corporeal reality' of man engaged in 'the concrete process of living' and relating to others. Towards the end of this section he concludes that 'ecclesiastical mysticism is proleptically oriented toward the totality of the Church' and that it 'admits not only spiritual but sensory experiences' (*GL1*: 414–15). But having explored the subjective evidence for faith, von

Balthasar is mindful of the danger of attempting to impose any kind of system upon God; 'all subjective evidence must remain exhaustively open to this freedom of the objective evidence of revelation' (*GL1*: 418). Thus, it is to the 'Objective Evidence' that von Balthasar will turn in the final part of his opening volume, *Seeing the Form.*

It is with this turn to the 'Objective Evidence' that we might expect some of the influence of Barth's christocentrism to shine through. Indeed it is no surprise to find a substantial section under the heading, 'Christ, the Centre of the Form of Revelation'. But this is only after von Balthasar has dealt with the 'Form of Revelation' in such a way as to confront both the 'Fact of Revelation' (in terms of the unity which Christ displays as 'Son of God' and as 'Word made Flesh') and its being a 'Revelation in Hiddenness'. It is in this latter section that von Balthasar seeks to deal with the tension between what is made manifest and what is hidden, for example between body and spirit, creation and creator, sinner and redeemer on the cross. His response, like many before him, is to affirm that God's form of revelation is one which also encompasses concealment, 'the revelation in the Incarnation has its place within the revelation of God's Being in man, who, as God's image and likeness, conceals God even as he reveals him' (*GL1*: 458–9). In this recognition of a 'dialectic of revelation and concealment' we can perhaps hear echoes of his earlier study of Barth in which, alongside the shift to analogy, there remains the ongoing influence of dialectical theology.

But for von Balthasar, this same tension points towards a different understanding, in that 'the evidence itself points to and indicates the nature of the *analogia entis* within itself' as 'the finite spirit finds itself directed by the analogy of Being beyond itself (since, as spirit, it is after all, finite Being) towards what can be "given" to its evidence only in the mode of non-evidence' (*GL1*: 450). He goes on to explore what this problem of 'concealment in revelation' might mean in terms of the classic definition of analogy offered by the Fourth Lateran Council, namely an 'ever-greater dissimilarity however great the similarity' (*in tanta similitudine major dissimilitudo*). This suggests that 'God's incomprehensibility is now no longer a mere deficiency in knowledge, but the positive manner in which God determines the knowledge of faith . . . This is the concealment that appears in his self-revelation; this is the un-graspability of God, which becomes graspable because it *is* grasped' (*GL1*: 461).

Having acknowledged the mystery which underlies God's revelation, von Balthasar now turns to the form it takes in Christ which he will deal with under three headings, namely the 'Centrality' of the Christ form, its 'Mediation' in the Scriptures and in the Church, and then its 'Attestation' in terms of the 'Testimony of the Father', of history and of the cosmos. Not surprisingly, it is in the section 'Christ the Centre of the Form of Revelation' that some of the themes which von Balthasar has identified in Barth come most clearly into view. For unlike the leaders and founders of other religions, Christ is both 'form' and 'content', indeed, 'Christ . . . is the form because he is the content'. Nor is his just a form to be studied and appreciated intellectually; 'What is at stake, rather, is the correspondence of human existence as a whole to the form of Christ' (*GL1*: 463–4).

But this means also that Christ's is a unique form, one which cannot be compared or contrasted with others, but can be measured only by itself. In part, this is because of the unique sense of 'attunement' or concordance between Christ's person and his divine mission (something which again will be developed further in the *Theo-Drama*). This gives to the Christ form a dynamism and fluidity of which Barth would approve, not least when von Balthasar uses language such as 'the dynamism of event' and refers to the Incarnation being understood 'no longer now as a state but as an event, or , if you wish, as the dynamic and eventful measuring of one's own static reality' (*GL1*: 473–4). Furthermore, von Balthasar is concerned to locate this dynamism of the Christ form within a trinitarian framework, and indeed quotes from Barth's *Church Dogmatics* IV.1 to support his position, which is that, 'In the Son of Man there appears not God alone; necessarily, there also appears the inner-trinitarian event of his procession; there appears the triune God, who, as God, can command absolutely and obey absolutely and, as the Spirit of love, can be the unity of both' (*GL1*: 479).

Moreover, as a unique form, the Christ form has also to be viewed in its entirety, in all its complexity and richness. It can not be perceived if there is an attempt to break it down into its component parts in the manner of the historico-critical method with its separation of the 'Jesus of History' from the 'Christ of Faith', or with Bultmann's project of demythologization. Nor can there be ignored the reality of hiddenness and concealment within divine revelation or the role of the Holy Spirit in enabling the Christ from to be perceived. Von Balthasar is not shy of comparing such disjointed, reductive approaches with what the early Church regarded as heresy. 'It is here that the problem of heresy has its roots; *hairesis*, the selective disjoining of parts' rather than an integrative approach in which 'every element calls for the other, and the more penetrating the gaze of the beholder, the more he will discover harmony on all sides' (*GL1*: 513). He is also clear that this can not happen without faith; what is required is 'con-version' – that is 'a turning away from one's own image and a turning to the image of God' (*GL1*: 522).

When it comes to his treatment of the 'Mediation' and 'Attestation of the Form', perhaps we shall not be surprised to discover that his exposition leads him to positions which are somewhat different from Barth's, particularly in their ecclesial implications. Von Balthasar's starting point is that such mediation and attestation are integral to the Christ-form itself. If 'His form is in the world in order to impress itself upon it and to continue to shape it', and 'We see what this form *is* from what it *does*', then this means that the matter of human agency, both in Scripture and in the Church, is not something which can be regarded as 'something external and alien to the Christ-form' but is rather as a vital and integral component of it (*GL1*: 527–8).

Scripture and Church share two important things in common; 'they are both perceptible expressions of the Christ-form (*corpora Christi*), but equally in both men share in their communication and formation' (*GL1*: 531). However, this remains a complex and overlapping relationship. As 'the canonical image of revelation, Scripture makes possible and guarantees the uninterrupted birth of the Church'. Indeed, it is not just scripture alone, for 'Scripture and Sacrament belong together and constitute the continual and unattenuated presence of revelation in the Church's every age' (*GL1*: 543). Von Balthasar is not against scholarly research and study of the Bible, whether in terms of the historico-critical or other forms of literary criticism; but what he insists upon is that these methods, with their supposedly neutral and objective approach, can not ultimately be sufficient to discern the form which Christ takes in scripture.

> This is why, in one sense, it is perfectly correct to say that the form of the historical Jesus (his preaching, for instance) which is discovered by the historico-critical method, is not and cannot be a form that is complete in itself and that satisfies faith; for it to unfold fully, it needs the sphere of ecclesial faith which really opens up only with Jesus' death and Resurrection. (*GL1*: 538)

Moreover, this insistence upon an ecclesial reading of Scripture leads on to the second aspect, which is the 'Mediation of the Form' in the Church. 'The Church is not Christ, but she can claim for herself and for the world no other figure than the figure of Christ, which leaves its stamp in her and shapes her through and through . . . ' (*GL1*: 559). It is at this point that we can discern how the mediation through the Church plays a very similar role as regards the 'Objective Evidence' in 'Seeing the Form', as does that of archetypal experience in von Balthasar's earlier account of the 'Subjective Evidence'.

Certainly many of the same key figures appear. There is the crucial role of Mary whose life offers 'the prototype of what the *ars Dei* can fashion from a human material which puts up no resistance to him' (*GL1*: 564), in whom is to be found 'the archetype of a Church that con-forms to Christ' which is 'Christ-bearing' or ' "Christophorous" in essence and actualisation' (*GL1*: 562) and who thereby offers, even to non-believers, 'a treasure of inviolable beauty'. There is the institutional office-bearing aspect of the Church, which finds its representation in the humiliation then exaltation of Peter and in the discovery of Paul that all his honour derives from the strength and weakness which come together in Christ's cross and resurrection. Outside of these personal experiences of the Apostles and their sharing in the life of the dying and rising Christ, for von Balthasar there remains no other basis to justify the form of the institutional Church and to render it plausible to the world.

Following on from this, von Balthasar goes on to explore how this form takes shape in the way that the Church is lived and experienced in the world; through the eucharistic cult, which exists 'as birth place and centre of the Church', through other sacramental events, for example baptism and confession, through the doctrinal and credal statements which embody the belief of the Church and enjoin obedience in those who believe, and finally through the Church's proclamation. It is not unexpected to find that proclamation and preaching have a much lower priority in the life of the Church than Barth allows in his *Church Dogmatics*. What is more of a surprise is to find that von Balthasar, for all his commitment to the life and form of the institutional Church, takes a similarly sceptical line to Barth as regards the practice of infant baptism. He regards it as 'inadequate as a model for the sacramental event' because 'the subject involved neither perceives nor understands Christ's gesture . . . a fact so conspicuously alien to Scripture (and to the baptismal practice of the Old Testament and of John) that it must without question be regarded as an exception' (*GL1*: 579).

Notwithstanding this proviso, von Balthasar's summary of this section is that 'in their power to express Christ, both Sacred Scripture and the holy Church together constitute the work of the Holy Spirit'; indeed they might have been entitled 'the testimony of the Holy Spirit' (*GL1*: 602). This points to the last major section of this opening volume in which he will deal with 'The Attestation of the Form' in terms of the testimony of the Father, of history (particularly of salvation-history as evidenced in the Bible) and of the cosmos.

The testimony of the Father draws heavily on the relationship between Father and Son which is witnessed in John's gospel. 'The Father is ground; the Son is manifestation. The Father is content, the Son form – in the unique way shown by revelation' (*GL1*: 611). For von Balthasar, this all points towards a trinitarian understanding of God, into which mystery it is the divine purpose to draw all believers. 'By his prayer and his suffering, the Son brings all his disciples – and through them all mankind – into the interior space of the Trinity' (*GL1*: 618).

The testimony of history looks at the relationship between Old and New Testaments as the eternal God in Christ enters human time; 'theological aesthetics culminates in the christological form (taking this word seriously) of salvation-history, in so far as here, upon the medium of man's historical existence, God inscribes his authentic sign with his own hand' (*GL1*: 646). This raises the issue of continuity across the biblical witness. Von Balthasar wants to affirm the basic unity of revelation to be found across both testaments; but for all the exploration of 'figure' and 'type' which can be found in the writings of Paul and of the Church Fathers, he is conscious too that the fullness of God's revelation in Christ is more than simply the fulfilment of what was promised in the Old Testament. Rather, the Old Testament points to something, or rather someone, beyond the conflicting categories and expectations of its own time, to a fulfilment which be seen and understood only in retrospect.

Finally the testimony of the cosmos refers to the way the divine glory is reflected in the response of the created order. It is revealed in the miraculous signs and authority over the powers evidenced during Jesus' ministry on earth and equally in the honour and glory accorded him in heaven. Both come to a climax in the resurrection. 'The same royal power, the same divine *kabod* (glory) is expressed in the dominion over creation as over the cosmic "powers," and at the resurrection what takes place is a simultaneous victory over both . . .' (*GL1*: 674). And in this vision of the divine glory, the angels too come to share; for 'just as the angels of the little ones on earth always behold the face of the Father for them in heaven (Mt. 18.10) so, too, men on earth behold for the angels the beauty of the God who has concealed himself in flesh' (*GL1*: 677).

So far in this chapter we have seen how von Balthasar has sought to restate the case for a properly grounded theological aesthetics which recovers a sense of the divine glory. We have suggested that in so doing von Balthasar has taken his starting point from Barth, both in terms of the rediscovery of the beauty of theology and its focus on Christ. We have also seen how von Balthasar will maintain that in order to do justice to its subject matter, his own *Theological Aesthetics* will seek to explore the glory of God not just as it relates to the divine revelation in Christ but as it also points towards the mystery of being itself, as beauty is viewed as one of the transcendentals of being, together with the good and the true.

All this has been done in some detail but only as regards *Seeing the Form*. This first volume is important because it establishes the principles which von Balthasar will use to develop his aesthetics and outlines the material which will be developed more fully in the later volumes. We will need now to look at how the material in these later volumes is developed in light of the approach set out in this opening volume. We shall not undertake for the remaining volumes the same level of detailed exposition which we have undertaken for this first one. But we will seek to establish both the structure of his argument and the themes which shape his material across the remaining volumes.

3.2 *STUDIES IN THEOLOGICAL STYLE: LAY* AND *CLERICAL STYLES*

Von Balthasar's concern is that the role of and desire for beauty has been lost. His particular concern in these two volumes is that this remains true even in the place where it should be most pre-eminent, namely Christian theology. Given his christological focus and insistence upon the importance of form, perhaps we should not be surprised to discover that he chooses 12 theologians from whom to explore how aesthetics can play its proper role in theology.

The reasons for the particular choices are outlined in his introduction. His aim is to present 'a series of Christian theologies and world-pictures of the highest rank, each of which, having been marked at its centre by the glory of God's revelation, has sought to give the impact of this glory a central place in its vision' (*GL2*: 13). There has been much discussion as to the rationale behind von Balthasar's selection, as he himself acknowledges, 'This is naturally, not to deny that, between these twelve figures picked out as typical, there is not a host of others who could have clarified the intellectual and historical relations and transitions between them and would in themselves also have been worthy of presentation' (*GL2*: 20).

Many of the names, in the first volume especially, are either giants of the Western tradition, such as Irenaeus and Augustine, or else those whom he has referred to extensively in the opening volume, such as Denys the Pseudo-Areopagite. Moreover, given the significance which von Balthasar recognises of Barth's study of Anselm, there is a particularly interesting section on Anselm's 'Aesthetic Reason'. But what is more significant for the purpose of this chapter is the way these studies are divided into two volumes under the headings, *Studies in Theological Style* first in terms of *Clerical* and then *Lay Styles*.

That there is more to this distinction than merely the matter of ordination becomes evident when, after the names of Irenaeus, Augustine, Denys, Anselm and Bonaventure in the second volume, we find included in the third, and supposedly 'lay' volume, the names of St John of the Cross, the Carmelite friar, and Gerard Manley Hopkins, the Catholic convert and Jesuit priest. Von Balthasar's introduction makes it clear why this should be. 'In the main we have chosen official theologians, so long as such were available, who were able to treat the radiant power of the revelation of Christ both influentially and originally, without any decadence; but after Thomas of Aquinas theologians of such stature are rare' (*GL2*: 15). The dividing line between the two volumes, which corresponds roughly to the year 1300, refers to the 'unfortunate but incontestable fact' that after this date, those who wish to assert the beauty and glory of the divine revelation find themselves in the position of being exiled and on the margins, almost an ecclesiastical 'opposition' 'protesting against a narrowing down of Christian theology merely to the training of pastors or to academic specialization and the timeless pursuits of the schools . . .' (*GL2*: 15).

St John and Hopkins have been chosen, together with the poet Dante, the mathematician and philosopher Pascal, the Lutheran pastor Hamann, the Russian theologian and writer Soloviev and the French novelist and poet Péguy, because each of them in their writings maintain a concern not just for the knowledge but also for the beauty of God. That their work must be categorized under the heading 'Lay styles' is for von Balthasar a reflection of the fact that in the Church for which they wrote, the concept of beauty had been lost within the accepted theology of their day. Sadly, this means that the vision which they offered was one which had to be maintained from the forgotten margins and perimeters of faith. Then marking the boundary between these two volumes, it is the role of Aquinas which von Balthasar identifies as crucial, as we shall see when we come to look at the next two volumes.

Irenaeus marks 'the birth of Christian theology' in which theology emerges as 'a reflection on the world of revealed facts' resulting in 'the miracle of a complete and organized image in the mind of faith' (*GL2*: 31). In countering the Gnostic mythology of Valentinus and others, Irenaeus is aware that he has to offer not just a rebuttal of their heresies but also a fuller and more complete version of the Christian truth. This means also that it is Irenaeus who offers 'the birth of theological form' in particular through the 'central concept' which governs his theology, namely *recapitulation* or *anakephalaiosis*, the summing up of all things in Christ (*GL2*: 51). Irenaeus' account of the creation and redemption of the world in and through Christ means that human nature 'has been taken into the divinely ordained Christian order' which 'also gives it proportion and beauty, and through it, the whole world' (*GL2*: 70). Moreover, from this comes 'the central concept of "glory" as the mutual glorification of God and man' (*GL2*: 74), that idea which we have already noted as a key influence upon von Balthasar as a result of his friendship with Henri de Lubac.

Augustine 'goes back to the aesthetics of the Christian era for which Irenaeus laid the foundations and extends it by integrating the periods of personal life into the massive construction of the ages of salvation-history' (*GL2*: 141). His theology is marked by that *eros*, that desire and yearning for a truth which can bring all things together in unity and which he finds in God. This quest is described both in his autobiographical and in his philosophical writings, which reflect on the key themes of 'the eye', 'light' and 'unity', and in which concepts such as 'harmony' and 'proportion' have their place. But ultimately such reflections culminate in his 'psychological images on the Trinity in the created soul' which 'form the conclusion not just of his metaphysics, but expressly, of his aesthetics' and from which considerations 'the beauty of all being is fully justified' (*GL2*: 134). Moreover they serve to inform the christological focus and thrust of his sermons; 'But how do we become beautiful? By loving him back, him who is eternally beautiful. The more love grows in you, the more beauty grows, since love is the beauty of the soul' (*GL2*: 136).

Denys 'can be regarded as the most aesthetic of all Christian theologians, because the aesthetic transcendence that we know in this world (from the sensible as manifestation to the spiritual as what is manifest) provides the formal schema for understanding theological or mystical transcendence (from the world to God)' (*GL2*: 168). For von Balthasar there remains something wonderful about the way in which this theology is revealed in someone who hides in pseudonymity (and whose work was unknown and ignored for centuries) and yet reveals an approach to theology which in focusing so clearly and exclusively on the divine shows up the shortcomings of any attempt to start from worldly realities. For Denys, 'Theology is exhausted in the act of wondering adoration before the unsearchable beauty in every manifestation' (*GL2*: 170) and in which 'holy measure' is enacted in 'holy celebration' (*GL2*: 172). Denys' theology is enacted in the liturgy of the Church, in which the 'hierarchy' is modelled on the divine 'thearchy' and so is 'not primarily graded subordination' but a 'divinely ordained divine order which leads to God and consists essentially of bounty and grace' (GL2: 202).

Anselm in his work 'realises in the purest form the concerns of theological aesthetics' (*GL2*: 211). His theology is not be accounted as primarily philosophical (as with some who have focused on the 'ontological' argument) or as juridical (as may appear from his account of the atonement) but are instead fashioned on what von Balthasar calls Anselm's 'aesthetic reason'. This understanding of 'the total (philosophical-theological) truth' demands '1. a life established on the truth and set free for it, to which there belongs for the Christian the wrestling of prayer; 2. the struggle for conceptual understanding so as to receive in-sight, *intel-lectus*; 3. the pure joy and blessedness (*delectatio, beatitudo*) in the truth thus found, which accrues to man through grace and merit alike. Each of these moments yields an aesthetic moment, from which the Anselmian *pulchritudo rationis* attains its unity' (*GL2*: 215). All this springs from the freedom of God, the 'utterly simple vision of the analogy between God and the creature as an analogy of freedom' (*GL2*: 237) from which it can be read that '*sponte* (freely) is the keyword of the Anselmian doctrine of redemption' (*GL2*: 243) in terms of God's saving grace in Christ.

Bonaventure is of all the great scholastic theologians 'the one who offers the widest scope to the beautiful in his theology' (*GL2*: 260). This originates in 'an experience of *overpowering* by the fullness of reality, like a sea that emanates gloriously from the depths of God, eternally flowing and not to be restrained' (*GL2*: 263). The major influence on his theology is Francis and this 'fundamental experience' of being overpowered by God is crystallized in 'the central image of the *stigmatisation of St Francis* on Mount Averna' (*GL2*: 270). For Bonaventure it is essential that the stigmata were branded upon Francis' body while his soul was in rapture; for 'it is when the form of the divine beauty is seen that this divine beauty receives its form in the world' (*GL2*: 273). It is also crucial that this is the form of the crucified

Christ, because Bonaventure goes on to describe 'the position of the Son within the Godhead not only as the place of truth but as the place of beauty' (*GL2*: 291) and in so doing opens the way towards an understanding of truth as one of the transcendentals of being.

Having looked at the significance of those 'Clerical styles' which offer a perspective from which beauty is still at the centre of the Church's theology, now is the time to look at those 'Lay styles' which seek to share that same vision but now from the margins of the Church.

Dante offers a new and unique perspective; not only is he a layman but he is writing in the vernacular, an innovation of the greatest historical significance both in literature and for theology. His *Divine Comedy* is 'a synthesis of scholasticism and mysticism, of Antiquity and Christianity, of the sacral concept of Empire and the spiritual Franciscan ideal of the Church' (*GL3*: 13). At the same time there is something irreducibly unique about Dante; he is 'the first to undertake the flight to heaven, although in Hell he follows in the footsteps of Virgil and Paul' (*GL3*: 12). His work gives 'precise formulation to what Thomas Aquinas quite deliberately left in suspense: the doctrine of the double end of man, earthly and heavenly' (*GL3*: 17). Dante's pursuit of Beatrice is an engagement with the existential issues of being human, with personality, destiny and *eros*. But what his journey reveals is two things at the same time; 'first the history of his redemption from perdition, his progressive realisation of what it means to be Christian; and second, his discovery of how his first and deepest love can become, in a Christian way, truly eternal' (*GL3*: 50).

St John of the Cross offers a response to the challenges posed both by Luther and the Reformation and by Columbus and the expansion of the known world. His response, drawing on the riches of the Eastern monastic tradition, is one which is even more radical than the Reformers could envisage. For John asserts the way of radical negation; 'God alone suffices' and 'All truths, every good and worthy object, anything that is not "God in himself" must be abandoned and transcended for the love of God' (*GL3*: 109). Yet this radical challenge is written in exquisite poetry; 'the reformer of Carmel responds to the negation of the Protestant reformers with beauty; to the destructive dialectical

Word with the constructive poetic Word' (*GL3*: 120). Out of the 'Dark Night' emerges 'the dawn of a new substantial delight in the ways of God, the beginning of transparent vision' (*GL3*: 139). But the crucial thing is that 'the world gains its beauty from above: from the divine love which . . . is the archetype of all beauty'. Moreover, 'the contemplative sees not only the beauty of God and in it the beauty of the world; he also sees in the moment of vision, as it were, the *analogia entis*' (*GL3*: 149).

Pascal is also read in terms of his response to the Reformation and the development in natural sciences. He shares too the inheritance of the Augustinian tradition, both in his insistence on the role of the *cor*, the heart, as the centre of human life and on the role of mathematics in approaching the beauty of God. This is 'the foundation of any doctrine of the beautiful in the Pascal of geometry and scientific experiments' (*GL3*: 188). Pascal also shared with Augustine the sense of that great chasm between the justice of God and the fallen nature of human being, a status characterized by 'divertissement' or separation. The only hope for restoration, or the *redire ad cor*, was to be found in grace, in Jesus Christ in whom is revealed 'the ever greater love of the incomprehensible God, and the sin of man that appears ever greater in its light' (*GL3*: 218). And so for Pascal, as for Augustine, 'the completed pattern of a Christian aesthetic must oscillate between the poles of the beauty of numbers and the beauty of grace as this is illuminated by the God who elects and rejects in a way beyond our understanding' (*GL3*: 188).

Hamann is the only Protestant figure in the list and is significant for the way in which he presents the case for an explicitly Christian aesthetic. Moreover, he does this in express and lonely opposition to the emerging forces of German idealism around him; 'it was Hamann's belief that the act of *aisthēsis* . . . is the original religious act itself, for all things are God's word and language . . . ' (*GL3*: 241). At the heart of this communication is God's self-emptying love in Jesus Christ, and so to 'understand Hamann and his aesthetics one must not stray too far from the miracle of "divine foolishness;" the whole world is a free descent by the divine spirit into the hells of createdness and materiality, and it is this very descent, this humility and poverty of God, that radiates forth in glory from all things' (*GL3*: 256). Hamann even allowed for the role of analogy ('The analogy of man to the

Creator bestows on all creatures their content and their form' (cited in *GL3*: 274)) but while his theology succeeds in bringing 'nature and supernature into a relationship of hiddenness and openness' (*GL3*: 276) in the end the inadequacies of his philosophical framework left him working in lonely isolation.

Soloviev the Russian intellectual is responsible for what has been termed 'the most profound vindication and the most comprehensive philosophical statement of the Christian totality in modern times', a system which according to von Balthasar 'aims at bringing a whole ethical and theoretical scheme to perfection in a universal theological aesthetic – a vision of God's coming to be in the world' (*GL3*: 281). Soloviev converted to Catholicism because he found in it a way of combining the need for the spirit to take objective form and the law of process; thus 'the total meaning of the world's evolution is clearly established for the future: the development of humanity and the totality of the world into the cosmic body of Christ' (*GL3*: 283). At the same time Soloviev drew on the Christian past, in particular Maximus the Confessor, whose theology makes the Chalcedonian formula the foundation upon which the entire structure of reality is erected. His fundamental idea is 'that, since Christ God has been given to men: that now it is man who is sought; everything from now on depends on the free acceptance of the grace of this gift – the "art" of the Kingdom at work, and the redemption of the cosmos' (*GL3*: 288).

Hopkins the English poet and priest represents a complete contrast to Soloviev, except in the matter of his conversion to Catholicism. For him it is not the universal which matters; rather in 'the unique, the irreducible there shines forth for Hopkins the glory of God, the majesty of his oneness, to whose ultimate, creative artistry the incomprehensibility of worldly images bears witness' (*GL3*: 357). Hopkins stands in the empirical tradition of Duns Scotus which emphasises the *haecceitas*, the individual form of specific things and is also influenced by the classics and the Greek concept of *kalokagathia* (the beautiful and the good). His poems combine these traditions with an acute love and study of nature and are characterized by two concepts; 'instress' which refers to the unique impression made and demanded and 'inscape' to the form which is revealed. Yet beyond this, they are also a response to the God who calls to him in Christ and this is the 'theological centre' from which Hopkins develops his laws of aesthetics. 'The principle lies in the fact that all truth is grounded in Christ, and that all beauty belongs to him, is related to him, is yielded to him in the "great sacrifice" and must rest with him' (*GL3*: 385–6). This is the 'doctrine of grace' that 'changed the natural doctrine of instress and inscape, for the true inscape of all things is Christ' (*GL3*: 387).

Péguy is the last of these 'lay' theologians and seeks an *approfondissement* or deepening of Christian faith. Péguy stands 'both inside and outside the church' and for him 'the shape that gives focus to everything is . . . the figure of Joan of Arc, that unique point of intersection of spiritual and secular action' (*GL3*: 405). But he was no narrow French nationalist; 'At the basis of the Christian demand to take root in the world lies the eternal concern of Israel, obscured by Platonism and recovered by Péguy' (*GL3*: 406). Nor could his aesthetic concerns be separated from political action, 'Peguy's concern was with a Christian aesthetic that could most easily be obtained through a Christian world revolution'. Moreover, 'Such an aesthetic would, for him, have to stand or fall by the "principle of hope," which in his earlier period he understands as the "principle of solidarity"' (*GL3*: 408). Ultimately, for Péguy this means committing himself to the future of the Church, but not the Church as it is, rather 'the Church in those places where the Church will be one day' (*GL3*: 404). And so, despite his personal unhappiness and disappointments, 'a man humbled in every way has been granted the privilege of uttering words, beyond all the fluency of theology to date, spoken as from the centre of God's fatherly heart, that reveal the glory of the *kenosis*' (*GL3*: 415).

3.3 THE REALM OF METAPHYSICS IN ANTIQUITY AND IN THE MODERN AGE

Von Balthasar's *Theological Aesthetics* is one which addresses the glory of God not just as it is perceived in revelation, but in terms of the beautiful as one of the transcendentals of being itself. For this reason his work cannot be restricted to the realm of theology alone; it must also deal with those aspects which are the concern of philosophy, particularly as philosophy was construed in the ancient world as the attempt to construct a framework of ultimate meaning or metaphysics. This is what von Balthasar attempts in *The Realm of Metaphysics in Antiquity*. In short, he will endeavour to show how Christian theology through the Church Fathers and into the Middle Ages sought to build on and offer a christological interpretation of the framework constructed by the classical pagan philosophers and poets.

The range of material from which he makes this argument is vast, and one which we can only intimate in outline. However, it is important that to recognize that von Balthasar's purpose in this is two-fold: in addition to his acknowledged apologetic thrust, as he seeks to interpret the biblical glory in terms of the resources of the classical tradition, he is also concerned to show how developments in the classical tradition can cohere within the metaphysical framework, based on the role of analogy and the transcendentals of being, which he has previously outlined in the opening volume, *Seeing the Form*. This requires a central role for analogy. 'It is only when there is an analogy (be it only distant) between the human sense of the divine and divine revelation that the height, the difference and the distance of that which the revelation discloses may be measured in God's grace' (*GL4*: 14).

Von Balthasar 'lays the foundations' for his approach in terms of three basic categories, namely, 'myth', 'philosophy' and 'religion'. Myth is that form which 'gives an interpretation of man in his relationship to the divine and thus gives him his being and his self-understanding'. Within this structure, there are two basic 'articulations': 'first, the irremovable separation of God and man and then man's transcendence into the sphere of God in which he finds his salvation, his greatness and his glory' (*GL4*: 45). Von Balthasar initially engages with the poetry of Homer, Hesiod and Pindar, in which the heroes of antiquity discover their destiny in terms of personal journeys and individual meetings with the gods. But in time, the focus shifts away from such glories and triumphs to the struggle to make sense of the divine will in the face of suffering and death. This is the subject matter of the great Attic tragedians, of Aeschylus, Sophocles and Euripides; but 'in tragedy the god is essentially remote' and 'the emphasis shifts to the one who is abandoned', to 'glory of the agonised heart which finally prevails, which endures more than could ever be asked of it . . . ' (*GL4*: 107).

Faced with this increasing remoteness of the gods, the ancient writers turned increasingly to 'philosophy', trying to find an explanation for the human condition through the use of human reason. However in order to do this, 'Reason, which wants to assure itself of the viability of its own transcendence into being, into the immutable, divine world, must at least "bracket off," methodically suspend, the act of glorifying God . . .' (*GL4*: 157). Thus in the philosophical writings of Parmenides, Heraclitus and Plato three new themes emerge: first, 'a claim to totality, a claim raised by knowledge'; then 'the ascent . . . in which philosophical knowledge itself is realised'; and finally 'that of harmony or proportion' which will in turn provide 'the key to the development of the philosophical notion of the beautiful . . .' (*GL4*: 164–5). Von Balthasar then explores in some depth how such themes are developed by Plato in particular.

Nevertheless, there remained a long period during which myth retained its hold on popular belief and ritual, while the intellectual framework which supported it became increasingly dependent on a philosophy which affirmed the role of human reason. This was the period dominated by 'religion', namely that 'synthesis between philosophy and myth' manifested in terms of a 'civic and domestic cultus' (*GL4*: 216). This synthesis was a particular challenge for the Roman Empire, a structure composed of so many different traditions and competing truth claims. It manifested itself in the civic religions of Seneca and Varro and in physical form in the Pantheon. But for von Balthasar, this synthesis was always under strain. 'It manifests itself as a bridge which is being thrown out from two piers on opposite shores and which seems all the time to be approaching the point where both constructions meet, yet always remains intrinsically incapable of being completed' (*GL4*: 216).

Yet there were two figures who would emerge at the end of Classical period and point a way forward for the future, namely the Roman poet Virgil and the philosopher-theologian Plotinus. Virgil's poetry shatters, or rather transcends, all the three categories just mentioned. From his poetry arises a 'radiant glow', 'a glow that arises from the poet's Yes to life in all its dimensions, the harsh and the beautiful', and a Yes which can only be uttered when it is 'a response to an ultimate, barely audible Yes on the part of being itself' (*GL4*: 261). Moreover, in Virgil's *Aeneid*, the story of how a family's flight from Troy presages the foundation of a new civilization, there emerges 'a form which puts him beyond all that had thus far been achieved in myth, philosophy and religion' and 'creates an analogy to Scripture in the ethical-aesthetic sphere' (*GL4*: 266). Christianity 'took as self-evident the interpretation of his love for the bringer of salvation, the divine child, the one who will establish the reign of peace, in terms of the Child who was to come into the world ten years after his death' (*GL4*: 278).

Similarly, Plotinus is 'the second figure who sums up the achievement of the old world and offers it to the new . . . '. For Plotinus 'being itself is the divine and its total revelation is for him so overwhelmingly glorious that it far outshines all the splendours of particular myths' (*GL4*: 280). Plotinus 'stands in awe and wonder before the glory of the cosmos' but for him 'Being, however, especially in so far as it encounters thinking is *form*'. 'Plotinus' aesthetic is founded on this statement: all being is beautiful because it is form, in its encounter with Intellect. The One is beyond being and Intellect and Form and Beauty, as their common source'(*GL4*: 294). Von Balthasar reflects on how, 'It is a rare and strange thing for a thinker both to draw together and bring to conclusion the themes of Antiquity and to open up the realm of Western philosophy . . . ' (*GL4*: 296) We can also see how useful such writings are for von Balthasar's construction of an aesthetic around form and the transcendentals of being.

Von Balthasar is aware that some will take issue with this method of engaging with Antiquity, and in particular with the notion that Christian theology must enter into dialogue with the human constructions of myth, religiosity and philosophy. He knows that there will be those 'announcing with Karl Barth in tones of loud conviction that Christianity is not a religion, or, with Kierkegaard, that it is not a philosophy, or, with Bultmann, that it is not a mythology. But God would not have become human if he had not come into positive inner contact with these three forms of thought and experience'. For von Balthasar, the conclusive evidence for his approach is found in the pages of the Bible itself. 'Paul quotes Aratos, John speaks of the Logos, the Epistle of James uses the convention of Stoic diatribe, the Deutero-Pauline letters take over the terminology of contemporary religious, cultic and political conceptions of *parousia* and *epiphaneia* without a trace of apprehension – to take only a few instances . . . '. His conclusion is that 'Those who want to "purify" the Bible of religion, philosophy and myth want to be more biblical than the Bible, more Christian than Christ' (*GL4*: 243–4).

Von Balthasar maintains that his approach is not just scriptural but one that is common to most theologians of the later patristic and mediaeval periods. For them it was very clear

> how the biblical glory of the Lord God could be thought and expressed in the categories of the ancient understanding of the glory of God and the world: and it was all the easier because this understanding was, in its very origins, a complete theology, which was only waiting to be purified in the Christian realm and then to continue its existence in a higher mode. (*GL4*: 320)

Thus the 'three great themes of Antiquity pass almost unbroken into the Christian: the theme of the procession and return of creatures from God and back to God', 'the theme of *eros* as the fundamental yearning of the finite creature for transcendence in God' and 'the beauty of the spiritual soul' (*GL4*: 321–2) and von Balthasar goes on to summarize this development in terms of the writings of Boethius, John Erigena and Alexander of Hales among others.

However, von Balthasar considers that this method reached its climax in the work of Aquinas. Previously in his study of Barth, von Balthasar had identified the pivotal role which Aquinas played in the history of theology, in that he sought to make sense of the yearnings of pagan philosophy and the classical world in the light of Christian revelation but in such a way as to establish a unified vision of reality around the transcendentals of being. Here in his *Aesthetics*, von Balthasar acknowledges that although 'Beauty is seldom a central concern for St Thomas Aquinas' (*GL4*: 393) nevertheless it is Aquinas' theological achievement which provides the basis for a theological aesthetic to be undertaken at all. It is his doctrine of 'the real distinction between *esse* and *essentia*' which 'enables us once again to make a clear distinction between the "glory" of God and the beauty of the world' (*GL4*: 395). According to von Balthasar, it is his distinction between *esse* and *essentia*, between that unique existence which pertains to God alone, and that sharing in being which is common to the rest of creation, which allows for the development of the analogy of being. And it is this understanding of analogy, enabling the whole creation to share in the divine beauty without being identified or subsumed within it, which, as we have seen, is central to von Balthasar's whole approach to theology.

Aquinas stands at a moment of transition, just as the schools start to assert their independence of the Church (fragmenting the relationship between theology and philosophy) and just as the study of theology separates from the practice of Christian spirituality. 'Thomas is a *kairos* in so far as ontology here shows itself to be a genuine philosophy', one which 'builds upon the "theological" ontology of the Greeks and early Scholastics who had understood being, together with its properties, as dynamically transparent to divinity'. But so too is his time; it represents 'an historically transient stage between the old monistic world of thought which, whether Greek or Christian, saw philosophy and theology as a unity and the approaching dualistic world which, whether Christian or non-Christian, will try to rend philosophy and the theology of revelation asunder and to make of each a totality' (*GL4*: 395–6).

For von Balthasar, it is the breakdown of that unified vision of reality which serves to undermine the role of the beautiful as one of the transcendentals of being. This represents the principal reason why aesthetics ceases to be a central focus for theology or philosophy, with all the disastrous results which von Balthasar will describe in his next volume, The *Realm of Metaphysics in the Modern Age*. In this he describes how the delicate balance which underpins Aquinas' metaphysics starts to unravel as the rise of the natural sciences leads to the assertion of the independence of human rationality from divine revelation. This is accompanied by a growing separation between the theology of the schools and the spirituality of the mystic tradition. All these developments have disastrous consequences for subsequent Christian metaphysics, which split off into different directions, described by von Balthasar as 'The Parting of the Ways'.

As in his previous volume, von Balthasar is dealing with a vast period of time and range of sources in a way which is both highly original and unusually ordered. He is not offering a history of

Western metaphysics; however, he is seeking to identify trains of thought which establish for him the crucial themes and decisions which must be taken for Christian theology to regain its bearings. To his mind there are 'three great movements'; the first is that of Scotus and Eckhart who, (with their descendants, Ockham on the one hand, Tauler and Nicholas of Cusa on the other) 'determine both the scientific and religious self-understanding of Europe'; the second is that of Luther and the Reformation which, 'itself standing on the shoulders of mysticism . . . offers its own shoulders to the third intellectual event, that which extends from Kant to Hegel and Marx' (*GL5*: 14). The scale and complexity of this volume makes it one of the hardest to read, and, with its strong 'Germanic' and 'literary' influences, no doubt reflects some of the studies which von Balthasar undertook for his doctoral thesis. All we can do at this point is to highlight the main themes and suggest why they are important.

The 'Parting of the Ways' begins with two developments (*GL5*: 16–47). On the one hand, there is the arrival of the Scotist tradition which insists that being is 'univocal', namely that 'being' is the same thing, whether applied to God or to humanity, and in turn renders it totally transparent and accountable to human rationality. On the other, there is the re-emergence through Eckhart of the mystic tradition, a tradition in which the individual is drawn into a relationship which blurs the distinction between divine and human so that, ultimately, being is held to be identical with God. In both instances the delicate balance which sustained Thomas' ontology is lost. In the one instance being is reduced to a dull and prosaic rationalism in which all sense of wonder and awe is lost; in the other, the sense of being lost in God becomes so all-embracing that any distinction between God and the world disappears.

There follows an extended section on the 'Metaphysics of the Saints' (*GL5*: 48–140) in which von Balthasar explores the impact on these developments on Christian spirituality, from the Rhineland mystics to the School of the Oratory. The emphasis derived from Eckhart's *Gelassenheit* (or 'abandonment') is marked by 'a clear choice of the Master's Christian life and a rejection of his speculative extravagances' (*GL5*: 51), a focus on individual devotion rather than metaphysics. Across this period, and perhaps reflecting on the experience of Adrienne von Speyr, von Balthasar acknowledges how from 'the Gothic period to the Baroque, *women* are prominent in spirituality' (*GL5*: 80) and engages with the writings of Angela of Foligno, Julian of Norwich and the two Catherines of Siena and Genoa among others. It is also noticeable that in von Balthasar's account it is only Ignatius, who though continuing with the idea of abandonment, did 'not adopt the metaphysical formulation given it by the German mystics' and maintained the ancient model 'whereby God is a form and the creature is matter' (*GL5*: 104). Ignatius thus 'achieves the inner synthesis of the two major parallel currents of the middle ages – scholasticism and mysticism' (*GL5*: 106).

Having examined this impact on metaphysics, von Balthasar's next section 'Folly and Glory' (*GL5*: 141–204) explores how such developments are also reflected in the understanding of humanity, particularly as revealed in literature. His conclusion is that 'one figure stands out', namely the 'real fool', the 'unprotected man, essentially transcendent, open to what is above him'. 'In the world of chivalry it is Parzival, in the age of humanism it is *The Praise of Folly*, in the Baroque it is Don Quixote and Simplicissimus', a long list joined by countess others 'from Shakespeare's comic and tragic fools (Hamlet, Lear with Edmund) to Kapellmeister Kreisler and Dostoievsky's *Idiot* and to Rouault, to Hofmannsthal, Chesterton and Unamuno' (*GL5*: 142–3).

According to von Balthasar, both these themes, the 'metaphysics of holy reason' (in the saints) and of 'foolish reason' (in literature) are attempts 'to short circuit the problem: they skipped the reality of the world which was left as a nominalist-positivist scene of wreckage and they sought divine glory in an immediate supernatural' (*GL5*: 206). However, there remains one last attempt to resolve the problem in Nicolas of Cusa who 'ties together in a knot the threads of the great Western tradition – Hellenism and Christianity, past and future' (*GL5*: 209). Nicolas' great strength is to articulate 'a vision of the unity of what in the context of the vision of reality found in Plotinus, Eckhart and the Bible may be manifest as "glory"' (*GL5*: 213). His weakness and what in the end undermines his attempt is that he 'projects the world-religions onto the background of the (Platonic-) philosophical and thus . . . sees in Christ above all the Logos, the perfect teacher of Wisdom'. The result is that 'the decisive glory of the God of Jesus Christ is emptied out' (*GL5*: 246) and the way paved for liberalism.

Faced with the weakness in Nicolas' programme, von Balthasar returns to what he has earlier termed 'the re-awakening of classical metaphysics' which reflects 'a cry to the *mediation of antiquity* for help by the Christian community threatened by the loss of the world' (*GL5*: 206). It is this great movement, which includes the rise of humanism in the fifteenth century, the Renaissance in the sixteenth, the Baroque in the seventeenth and then the Enlightenment and German Idealism from Winckelmann to Schiller and Goethe, and then to Schelling and Hegel in the eighteenth and nineteenth centuries, that is the subject of his next major section, 'Classical Mediation' (*GL5*: 247–450). It is a subject area close to von Balthasar's heart in light of his earlier academic studies and one he regards as 'one of the most glorious periods of human history'. But it is also one 'stirred up by the inner contradiction to two mutually cancelling spiritual fields of force', namely that 'cry for help to classical piety' and at the same time 'a bold storming ahead on the ways of thought which Christianity had certainly opened up, but only to those who would treat them in faith and in love' (*GL5*: 247). This long section includes some moving passages and tributes to the 'mysteriously radiating glory' revealed in Michelangelo and Hölderlin, in Goethe and in Rilke. But it ends with Heidegger, whose philosophy of Being 'identifies the negations of the classical, Christian doctrine of God . . . with the nothingness of the act of Being which constitutes world' and thus loses the *analogia entis* which preserves the distinction between God and world in an *identitas* which embraces and envelopes both (*GL5*: 447).

This risk is heightened in the third and final stage in the process, which von Balthasar accounts for in 'The Metaphysics of Spirit' (*GL5*: 451–596). He seeks to show how the individual and pietist concerns of the mystic tradition are picked up together with the existential concerns concerning judgement and damnation which formed the backdrop to Luther and Protestant Reformation, leading to a stress upon personal salvation and assurance of grace rather than any wider metaphysical framework. The philosophical writings of Descartes, with its emphasis upon the knowing and thinking subject, and then Spinoza and Leibniz, pave the way for the for Idealism in its modern and German context. Here von Balthasar shows how, building on the framework of Kantian metaphysics, the writings of Fichte and Schelling come to focus on the rational subject, the supreme 'I', as the only basis for knowledge and belief. Their approach wants 'to conceive of man within the wholeness of the Absolute, as its centre' (*GL5*: 547). But in so doing, ' "critical Idealism" no longer permits space for an experience of worldly Being as an epiphany of God's glory' (*GL5*: 483). The logical progression of this is the emergence of an idealist dialectic, whether in terms of the supreme spirit or mind in Hegel, or alternatively the materialist reductionism of Marx.

In all these developments von Balthasar sees the loss of that concept of form and beauty which is grounded on an analogical concept of being. It is replaced by an inadequate philosophical framework, in which all distinction is lost as everything merges together in an undifferentiated unity or identity and there is no place left for glory. This is a consequence of the loss of that unified concept of being provided by Thomas' ontology.

> 'Glory' stands or falls with the unsurpassability of the *analogia entis*, the ever greater dissimilarity to God no matter how great the similarity to Him . . . . In so far as German Idealism begins with the *identitas entis*, the way back to Christianity is blocked; it cannot produce an aesthetics of 'glory' but only one of 'beauty': and the 'aesthetics as science', which was rampant in the nineteenth century, is its fruit. (*GL5*: 548–9)

It is significant that here we have returned to von Balthasar's criticisms of Idealism and its metaphysics of identity which was crucial to his critique of Barthian theology. According to von Balthasar it was this metaphysical deficiency that accounted for the shift in Barth's theology from dialectic to analogy, although he did not believe Barth's 'conversion' was as complete as it needed to be. In his own theology von Balthasar will insist upon an analogical understanding of being is the only basis for a biblical understanding of divine glory. So it is back to the biblical witness that he returns for the final two volumes of *The Glory of the Lord.*

3.4 *THEOLOGY: THE OLD AND NEW COVENANT*

Von Balthasar has already set out the outline for his programme in his opening volume *Seeing the Form.* He will seek to demonstrate how the Old and New Testaments must be seen as part of the one witness to the divine glory, even though the nature of the different strands within the Old Testament testimony is such that they cannot be fully understood, except in so far as they point beyond the boundaries of their own experience and understanding to that witness born in the New Testament to the Word made flesh.

However, as von Balthasar develops his account, it is worth noting how his exposition of the divine glory is influenced by that section in Barth's *Church Dogmatics* II.1 dealing with 'The Eternity and Glory of God'. As another commentator notes, *The Old Covenant* begins, with von Balthasar 'at his most Barthian' (Nichols 1998: 188). The beginning and end of Christian religion is the gracious self-communication of the totally other God. The fact that this evokes a human response in terms of a 'fear of the Lord' and a 'commitment to love our neighbour', does not detract from the fact that it originates solely from the revelation of God. 'There is no dodging this paradox, which begins with the self-communication of the Wholly Other and ends with the thanksgiving of the creature that has been overtaken' (*GL6*: 10). To suggest anything else, as von Balthasar himself acknowledges, 'would rightly fall victim to the criticism of Karl Barth'.

If God speaks his word to created men and women, surely it is because he has given them an understanding which, with God's grace, can achieve the act of hearing and comprehension. But if it is really *God's* word and self-communication that they are to hear and understand, then this can surely not occur on the basis of a neutral foreknowledge of what "words" mean or what "truth" is. Such encounter with God cannot take place on a dialogical plane which has been opened in advance; it can only occur by virtue of a primary sense of being overawed by the undialogical presupposition of the dialogue that has started, namely the divinity or glory of God. (*GL6*: 11)

(It is this understanding which the German title of his work conveys in a way which the English translation cannot match, for it combines both the aspects of 'sublimeness' (*Hehrsein*) and 'lordliness' (*Herrsein*) within the 'glory' (*Herrlichkeit*) of the self-communication of God.)

It also means that such a biblical theology will have liturgical and ecclesial implications, as well as an impact on Christian art;

liturgical because 'God's demonstration of his glory is always necessarily answered by the glorification (doxology) of God' and will thus be reflected in Christian worship; ecclesial, and indeed ecumenical, on the presumption that 'the dogmatics of the Orthodox, Evangelical and Catholic churches in each case has its centre in the concept of the *Gloria Dei* and that, consequently, a fruitful dialogue among these churches can be conducted only starting from this common centre' (pointing towards the final volume of his *Aesthetics* which was never written); and finally in terms of Christian art, since it is in the Bible that 'the forms and branches of the artistic domain are in various ways made serviceable to revelation' (*GL6*: 24–7).

Von Balthasar then goes on to examine this self-communication of God under three headings, namely 'glory', 'image' and 'grace and covenant'. His use of these themes corresponds to the approach set out in *Seeing the Form*, in which a theological aesthetics requires both a theory of vision, reflecting on the splendour of the objective form to be perceived, and a theory of rapture, in which the human recipient is transformed and drawn into the divine glory, as evidenced in the heading, 'God's Glory and Man'. In his treatment of the divine glory or *kabod* of God in the Old Testament (*GL6*: 31–86), von Balthasar groups these experiences of the presence of God under three headings; those theophanies which are part of the salvation-history of Israel (such as the events on Sinai), those which relate to the experience of being called by the prophets (for example Isaiah and Ezekiel) and those which are interpreted through the cosmos as part of the wisdom tradition (in Job and the Psalms). However, these forms, the 'historical', the 'prophetic' and the 'cosmic' cannot be too sharply demarcated.

> The three forms are integrated beyond separation. In the theology of Israel, the historical experience of God occupies first position, serving as foundation for everything else; this experience primarily presents itself as including a sensory element, and then for further clarification, it draws on both natural and mythical images. The prophetic experience, as Habakkuk has shown, can blend inseparably with the historico-natural experience, and the vision of God's glory is at bottom the vision of those who know God's historical word

and action and who, with enlightened eyes, see the Creator in the creation . . . . (*GL6*: 85)

In his next section on the 'image', (*GL6*: 87–143) von Balthasar focuses upon humanity, as the partner whom God has created for himself to share in a portion of his glory. Here again von Balthasar picks up on themes which he has set out earlier. 'The beautiful does not live on splendour alone; it also needs figure (*Gestalt*) and image (*Bild*) even if what figure (*Ge-stalt*) does is attest to him who set it up . . . ' (*GL6*: 87). But his treatment in this section also leans heavily on Barth's anthropology and interpretation of the *imago Dei* in Genesis 1, namely that humanity is to be God's co-respondent partner in creation. Human beings have a share with God in dominion over the rest of creation, and von Balthasar is to explore how the stories of Israel's kings, David and Solomon, reflect something of the archetypal experience of the kingly rule of God, as does the courtly wisdom of Proverbs and the sage reflections of Ecclesiastes . But it also means that 'the creature is also granted a certain space to be at home within itself before God; indeed, a sphere of autonomy is allowed it over against God that it may be a "world" of its own with respect to God' (*GL6*: 88). For at the same time the creature is created by and for God, and this leads onto the third theme which is to do with that which governs the relationship between God and creature, namely 'grace and covenant'. Von Balthasar himself acknowledges where his treatment of the relationship between the two comes from; for 'Karl Barth has captured this priority in the now classical formula that says that creation (and, with it God's image in man) is the outward ground of the covenant and the covenant, in turn, is the inner ground of creation' (*GL6*: 88 note 3).

This leads naturally to the third theme of 'grace and covenant' (*GL6*: 144–211) and here von Balthasar explores how this relationship of divine revelation and human response takes a distinct and yet representative form as interpreted through the *berith* or covenant that God makes with Israel. This is not an 'equal' relationship, 'It is two-sided because it is based on the one-sidedness of the love of God that makes election' (*GL6*: 156). It is not an equal relationship also because what is revealed on God's side of the covenant in terms of faithfulness, righteousness, justice and mercy is met by the fact that 'Israel will not be able to sustain this "I-Thou" relationship. It will break the covenant' (*GL6*: 158), and from this failure 'there grows the figure of the mediator, the vicarious representative who prays and suffers' (*GL6*: 189). All this means that the covenant 'requires us to reach back into prehistory and primal history (provenance, Genesis) and to reach forward into existence alongside other peoples and the world . . .' because 'ultimately, Israel exists not for itself, but for the world' (*GL6*: 192–3).

Von Balthasar then has to explain how these themes, which allow Israel, and through Israel all humanity, to share in a portion of the heavenly glory, also allow for the breakdown of that covenant relationship and the reality of evil. For von Balthasar, this is the role of the prophets, witnessing to the encounter between evil and the divine glory, a foretaste of that deeper conflict which will be experienced on the Cross (*GL6*: 225–98). In the midst of all that threatens to shadow and hide the glory of God, von Balthasar finds three elements in the closing pages of the Old Testament which point beyond the darkness to the glory which is to come. There is 'messianism' ('Glory ahead') which looks beyond the experience of present impotence to a new and glorious king (*GL6*: 305–20); there is 'apocalyptic' ('Glory above') which looks beyond earthly suffering to a heavenly kingdom and resurrection (*GL6*: 321–43); finally there is 'wisdom' ('Glory anticipated') which, encouraged by the growing influence of Greek philosophy upon Jewish thought, looks beyond the historic tradition to see the signs of God's immanence in the surrounding cosmos (*GL6*: 344–64).

All of these are ways in which Israel seeks to preserve glimpses of the glory of God in troubled times. However the reality is that the post-exilic period has become a time 'without glory', a period that von Balthasar calls 'empty time', when the glory of God is 'covered by a thick veil' (*GL6*: 366). There are attempts to fill this time with two further developments; first the 'speech event' which seeks to preserve the original revelation of God on Sinai in terms of a meditation and interpretation of the Mosaic law (*GL6*: 375–87), and secondly the 'blood event' in terms of sacrificial system and cultic worship at the Temple (*GL6*: 388–401). But in each case they point to a fulfilment which can not be comprehended within the thought forms or framework from which they come. From von Balthasar's perspective, the witness of Israel viewed as a whole in *The Old Covenant* points towards what is to yet to be, as the only way of interpreting that which can not be fully comprehended within its own tradition. And what they point to is the subject of the next and final volume, *The New Covenant*.

Von Balthasar's introduction to this final volume recognizes it to be the climax of *The Glory of the Lord*, 'We make ready with nervousness to scale the final slope, the ascent which was the goal of all the earlier advances forward'. For the task which is set is to 'describe the ineffable final matter of the definitive meeting which unites God and man (the world), and here least of all we can forego the concept of "form"' (*GL7*: 13–14). Moreover, it is significant that here again in his introduction he acknowledges how his approach is influenced by Karl Barth. He offers a summary of Barth's treatise on God's glory in the *Church Dogmatics* II.1; Glory is 'God himself in the truth, in the capacity, in the act which he makes himself known as God': this comes to fulfilment in Christ who is both the perfect image of the glory of the Father and 'the archetype of all creaturely participation in the glory of God': from this derives our concept of beauty in that 'we speak of the beauty of God only to help in the explanation of his glory' and it is this, rather than any general or metaphysical concept of beauty which provides the basis for a biblical-theological aesthetics (*GL7*: 21–2).

Von Balthasar acknowledges that Barth does not offer an aesthetics which runs throughout his *Dogmatics*. Instead he offers three central examples as to how the glory, and thus beauty of God is to be known: first in 'the wonderful unity – now puzzling, now clear in itself – of identity and non-identity, of simplicity and multiplicity, of inner and outer, of God himself and the fullness of that which he is as God'; second as this becomes visible at a deeper level in the relationships of the Trinity of order, relationship and form, so that 'the Trinity of God is the mystery of his beauty'; thirdly as the Trinity comes into view for us in the Incarnation as the 'centre and goal, and thus also the hidden beginning of all God's ways' so that in Jesus Christ 'God's beauty embraces death as well as life , fear as well as joy, that which we would call ugly, as well as that which we would call beautiful' (*GL7*: 22–3). Moreover, von Balthasar sketches Barth's outline 'not only because it agrees with our overall plan, especially as regards the relationship between glory and beauty, but also because it offers at the beginning an overview that we ourselves can approach only slowly'.

For von Balthasar's aim is to construct a theology of the new covenant in which, as with the old, 'Everything is ordered around the guiding concept of glory' (*GL7*: 23–4). This project is one which will be undertaken in three parts.

> First we must speak of the matter itself, which bears the name not of "glory," but of Jesus Christ; then we must follow on to speak of the application of the affirmation of glory to him and to all that concerns him; and third, we must speak of the response of the world, as this is changed in the New Testament – the glorification of the glory. (*GL7*: 27–8)

However, and in light of the previous volume, the significance is that he is here offering 'a new formulation of the *argumentum ex prophetia*' (*GL7*: 33). His argument is that,

> Judaism's three forms of reaching out for the missing glory of God can find a home in the unity of the new covenant only by way of their total dismantling. The image of the coming Messiah must be broken through the image of the suffering Servant of Yahweh . . . apocalyptic must undergo a complete transformation of signification, and be humbled to the role a function of the dying and rising of the man Jesus; the sapiential teaching can be utilised only when it lets itself be measured against, and brought into alignment with, the scandal of the Cross and of the "foolishness of God" that appears therein – for the "lord of glory" must be crucified (1Cor. 2.8). (*GL7*: 39)

It is in the first section entitled *Verbum Caro Factum*, 'the Word made flesh' (*GL7*: 33–235) that von Balthasar deals with 'the matter itself' or what might otherwise be termed the 'event' of the Incarnation. He engages with the announcement of Jesus' coming by the Baptist, the accounts of his birth, his infancy and his temptation, and the role of his mother, Mary. His assessment of the Magnificat typifies the approach which he has adopted; 'the Magnificat is the expression of the summary of Israel's history . . . as its fulfilment breaks in, in the impulse of the transcendence which God alone can introduce to elevate its whole meaning' for 'in Mary, the faith of the covenant partner finds its embodiment' (*GL7*: 62). He reflects on the paradox of how it is that the Word of God becomes wordless, when 'in the midpoint of this one word stands death, in which his word becomes a cry and falls silent' (*GL7*: 90) and on the 'indissoluble nexus between event (Christ) and interpretation (Church)' (*GL7*: 115). He identifies the fundamental characteristics of Jesus' life and ministry in terms of his 'authority', 'poverty' and 'self-abandonment' and shows how this 'kenotic' theme is manifested in the life of the Church in word and sacrament.

Subsequently in the 'Momentum of Time' and the 'Momentum of the Cross' he explores how Jesus' example serves to shape the Christian understanding of life and death. In terms of time, 'The Jesus who was with us imprints on the time of the Church his own form, the form of the one who became lord of all time through the perfecting of his temporality' (*GL7*: 181) and in terms of bridging the 'hiatus' caused by human sinfulness in light of the Cross, 'the only right approach to the mystery is to see the whole momentum of "God's wrath" in the Old Testament over the broken covenant as taken up into the far greater momentum of the love of God in the New Testament – the love of the Father as well as the Son . . .' (*GL7*: 205). This is why 'in John the raising up upon the Cross and the raising up into glory are one single event, just as for Paul no one is raised up apart from the one who was crucified' (*GL7*: 228). In both instances, von Balthasar is keen to draw attention to 'the momentum of the call to unconditional discipleship' (*GL7*: 188), for it is through such discipleship, enabled by the grace of God in Christ, that the divine glory is also to be revealed. 'The grace of following belongs to the "glory" of the momentum of the sole Cross' (*GL7*: 201).

In the second section *Vidimus Gloriam Eius*, 'We have seen his glory' (*GL7*: 239–385), von Balthasar explores the ascriptions of 'glory' in the New Testament, an ascription which occurs 116 times as a noun and more than 60 times as a verb. The fact that the title is taken from the prologue to John's Gospel reflects von Balthasar's view that in the Johannine tradition is found the fullest and deepest contemplation upon 'the trinitarian mutuality in giving honour, in bringing to recognition, in "glorifying"'

(*GL7*: 246). This is where his account begins with the mutual glorification of Father and Son in Chapter 17 of John's Gospel. But there is also the Johannine theme of fruitfulness, as the cruci-fied Christ is glorified in the Church, for Jesus 'has succeeded in revealing the Father's love in such a way than men have accepted it' and thus 'the divine love has taken root on earth' (*GL7*: 259).

Having begun with John, in whom *doxa* or glory operates as a governing motif for the whole gospel, von Balthasar then goes on to explore how this same theme figures throughout the rest of the New Testament corpus, not least in the writings of Paul, for whom it has a similarly central role in, for example, 2 Corinthians 4.6: 'It is the same God who said "Let light shine out of darkness," who has shone in our hearts, to give us the knowledge of the glory of God upon the *face* of Christ' (*GL7*: 264). However, with Paul comes a 'new and final level' in the understanding of glory 'characterised by the kinship between *glory and righteousness*' and with this 'the central theme of Paul's theology takes its place in our theological aesthetics' as 'the pre-sentation of the contents of glory attains its highest point' (*GL7*: 297). Von Balthasar also addresses the 'hidden glory' of God, particularly as this is found in the Synoptic gospels, noting for example how glory is often associated with apocalyptic expecta-tions of the Son of Man, how the 'messianic secret' operates through Mark's gospel and how, despite the ascriptions in some of the epistles, the aspect of glory is lacking in the gospel accounts of the resurrection, to which he refers as the 'hidden Easter'. Yet it is to Paul and John that von Balthasar returns at the end of this section as he reflects on how,

> Where the hiddenness of Christ's glory is concerned, it is but a step from Paul to John. There is a distance – for Paul the earthly life of Jesus is without glory, while John lets the glory shine though everything, Incarnation, miracles and passion – but this distance is not great, because, as has been shown, the life of Jesus makes sense and comes to light in his Cross, which however takes on its inner meaning only from the light of the Resurrection. (*GL7*: 368)

In his final section *In Laudem Gloriae*, 'To the praise of his glory' (*GL7*: 389–543), von Balthasar addresses the Christian response to the glory which has been revealed. His starting point is that of Jesus in John's gospel, in which not only is glory given by the Son to the Father but also shared with the disciples whom the Son has chosen. So too the followers of Christ are to offer back glory to God, and in so doing come to share in that life and relationship which belongs to the Trinity of Father, Son and Holy Spirit. But this offering back of glory is not restricted to praise and thanksgiving in worship alone; glorification involves all aspects of Christian life and service. Sharing by the power of the Spirit in the life of Christ through which the glory of God the Father has been revealed, 'we must praise him through our existence, inasmuch as this is an existence that is in him and therefore what it truly ought to be: an existence in the love that hands itself over' (*GL7*: 397).

This 'pneumatology of Christian existence' is explored by von Balthasar under the headings 'Appropriation as Expropriation' and 'Giving back the fruit to God'. The first relates to that 'exchangeable formula' found in Paul; 'it can be said both that "Christ lives in me" or "in us" . . . and that we are, or live, or are found "in Christ"' and 'the reciprocity involved remains not only formal but substantial: the purpose of the indwelling is an existence *for* the other . . .' (*GL7*: 407). But equally important is the image of 'fruitfulness'; it is 'a dominant idea which runs through the whole of the New Testament' and its 'evident connection with "glorification" is explicitly set out in the image of the vine: "My Father is glorified when you bear much fruit" (Jn 15.8)' (*GL7*: 416). And crucially it means that this is not some thing which Christians can undertake as individuals alone; it will also involve the Church. 'The miracle of God's glory, which was the goal projected for all things at the beginning, is truly revealed in this restitution of grace, as the Church's love, through the brethren to God: the man who believes and loves has substantially become "the glorification of the glory of the grace" of God (Eph. 1.6)' (*GL7*: 431).

It is in the next section, under the heading 'The Brother for whom Christ died' that von Balthasar draws out the fundamentally ecclesial nature of this process of glorification. His argument is 'to suggest the necessity of incorporating the Church, and through her the world, more strongly into the christological and trinitarian disclosure of absolute being' (*GL7*: 432). He does this by exploring three themes in turn: 'Encountering God in one's brother' reflecting on how the command to love God and love neighbour is established in Christ's sacrificial death on the Cross; 'Solidarity' in terms of the 'Communion of Saints' and the fact that 'it is only the Church in the love of Christ and of God that remains as the surpassing model of solidarity' (*GL7*: 469); and 'Nuptiality' in that the Church is called to be not only the Body but the Bride of Christ. 'In the Church, humanity is given a face for God. She is the body that is given its form by the Spirit and the blood of God and of Christ, only because at the same time she is his bride and his spouse' (*GL7*: 484).

All this means that 'since Jesus prays to the Father to permit those who belong to him to dwell where he is and to see his glory (Jn 17.24) and the Church is already the place where he is, the personal and social life of the Church permits one to see into the glory of Christ and of the triune love' (*GL7*: 467). It is the Church which embodies the solidarity between fellow Christians, in terms of recognizing in our fellow humans the brother for whom Christ died. Moreover, as the Spirit bears fruit in the life of the Church and enables the transformation of wider human society, so too it is the Church which embodies hope for the world. She bears witness in her life and her worship to the now and not yet, in the story of cross and resurrection which includes Good Friday, Holy Saturday and Easter Sunday. And ultimately she points to the way in which all things will be taken up into the glory of God.

For as in his study of Barth, so too in his *Theological Aesthetics*, it is to a christologically centred Church that von Balthasar allows his last word.

> The risen Lord too is once more a visible form, but one that has passed through the gulf of the abyss. And it is precisely from the risen Lord that the earthly visibility of the Church has her soul and her spirit, so that she has as it were a form that is already alien to the world that is passing away, a form that has its home elsewhere . . . . Put more precisely, she is the response of glorification, and to this extent she is drawn into the glorious Word to which she responds, and into the splendour of the light without which she would not shine. What she reflects back in the night is the light of hope for the world. (*GL7*: 543)

CHAPTER 4

THEO-DRAMA: THEOLOGICAL DRAMATIC THEORY

INTRODUCTION

The *Theo-Drama* is the second part of von Balthasar's great trilogy. It consists of some 5 volumes and more than 2000 pages, originally published over a ten-year period between 1973 and 1983, and represents a massive theological undertaking in its own right. Indeed for many scholars, it marks the high-point of von Balthasar's work. In a *Festschrift* to mark von Balthasar's 80th birthday (involving many of those who translated *The Glory of the Lord*) the editor John Riches wrote that; 'Balthasar's own most sustained theological reflections are to be found in the second part of his projected trilogy, *Theodramatik*' (Riches 1986: 192). In similar vein, Edward Oakes, the translator of *The Theology of Karl Barth*, has written that,

> I regard the last three volumes of the Theodramatics as the culmination and capstone of his work, where all the themes of his theology converge and are fused into a synthesis of remarkable creativity and originality, an achievement that makes him one of the great theological minds of the twentieth century. (Oakes 1994: 230)

Von Balthasar himself makes it clear that this work has been planned as the middle- piece of a 'triptych' or trilogy. The opening volume of the *Theo-Drama* sets the scene with an examination of the role of 'Dramatic Theory between Aesthetics and Logic', offering a rationale for why the *Theo-Drama* follows naturally on from *The Glory of the Lord*. The 'theological drama' has already begun with the *Aesthetics,* since 'catching sight' of the glory is inconceivable without being 'transported' by it. But perceiving, indeed being enraptured by the form, is only a prelude to getting involved, and here von Balthasar may have been conscious of criticism that his approach has so far been contemplative and quietist. 'For God's revelation is not an object to be looked at: it is his action in and upon the world, and the world can only respond, and hence "understand", through action on *its* part' (*TD1*: 15).

The *Theo-Drama* is where we get down to the action. In terms of von Balthasar's grand scheme of approaching theology in terms of the transcendentals of 'being', the beautiful, the good and the true, it will be concerned with the *good*, for that is at the heart of what God has done for us in Christ, just as his *Aesthetics* dealt with the *beautiful*, with the glory of the divine Word. But it is not a good to be observed passively.

> The *good* which God does to us can only be experienced as the *truth* if we share in *performing* it . . . ' and this is possible because God 'has already taken the drama of existence which plays on the world stage and inserted it into his quite different "play" which, nonetheless, he wishes to play on our stage. It is a case of the play within the play: our play "plays" in his play. (*TD1*: 20)

It is this divine but humanly involving drama of salvation which will be the subject of the *Theo-Drama*.

Given von Balthasar's recovery of a theological role for the aesthetic in *The Glory of the Lord*, his own academic background in German literature and philosophy, and his lifelong interest in culture and the arts, perhaps we should not be surprised at his adoption of such a literary approach. Admittedly, his initial encyclopaedic survey of dramatic form and theory across the centuries in Volume I has to acknowledge that the Church's attitude towards theatre and the acting profession has at best been ambivalent. But at the same time, as other commentators including Oakes have noted, this very ambivalence leaves von Balthasar with a great deal of relatively unexplored material to shape and use in his own highly original and distinctive way.

4.1 *PROLEGOMENA*

In Volume I, the *Prolegomena*, von Balthasar seeks to establish the dramatic resources which will be used in his theological dramatic theory. Prior to this, he first identifies some nine trends in modern theology which may also prove serviceable to his enterprise (*TD1*: 25–50), although he recognizes that an over-emphasis upon any one will only serve to distort the theological enterprise as a whole. The first of these categories is that of 'event', and here von Balthasar engages quite explicitly with the thought of both Bultmann and the 'young Barth'. There is a proper concern for the 'here and now', the *kairos* of God's appointed hour, but this does not mean that all of time is to submerge into the one decisive event.

> Here the vertical event has unfolded into a series of times of salvation comparable to the acts of a play . . . It is not as if there is *only* the fifth act, or even *only* the crucial scene of the peripeteia: God plays the whole piece right through with the individual human being and the human race. (*TD1*: 28)

Following on from this, von Balthasar warns against going to the other extreme. There is also a proper concern for 'history', but against this, he warns against any understanding of history that fails to appreciate the decisive significance of God's revelation in Christ and seeks to interpret this as a series of unfolding acts over time. Other important themes which he identifies include: the concern for 'orthopraxy', for right practice in response to the glory, the *doxa* of God (perhaps revealing a sensitivity to allegations made against the contemplative mode of his *Aesthetics*); for 'dialogue' as an approach to truth; for 'political theology' in terms of engagement with the world; for 'futurism' in rediscovery of the importance of eschatology and for 'function' in response to the challenges and insights of structuralism. With most of these trends we sense that von Balthasar has some, but only limited sympathy. However with the last two, we arrive at themes which will play a crucial role throughout the *Theo-Drama*, namely the concept of 'role' and personality, and the problem of 'creaturely freedom', including the 'possibility of evil'. It is von Balthasar's conviction that a properly theo-dramatic theory will have a better chance of holding all these disparate concerns together in a theological whole than alternative approaches have hitherto managed.

Von Balthasar then addresses some 'objections' which have been raised against the idea that there can be an analogy between the dramatic, or at least the theatre, and Christianity. On the one hand he addresses the writing of Hegel who maintained that Christianity had abolished art (and drama as the highest form of art), and his influence on Marx and Engels with their emphasis upon a scientific (and materialistic) determinism which left no room for a drama requiring human engagement. On the other hand, he addresses the complex and often hostile attitude which the Church has had towards the theatre from the time of Tertullian onwards, recognizing that this relationship has been a 'lively and sometimes stormy one' (*TD1*: 87). In addition to deeper theological concerns about 'play-acting' and 'performing roles', von Balthasar also recognizes that there have been long-standing practical and moral concerns about the licentiousness which can accompany festivals and theatre, and which have surfaced throughout Church history from the time of early Church synods to the Protestant reformers and the eighteenth-century Papacy. But at the same time there is also a long tradition of religious drama, from medieval mystery plays to the eucharistic liturgies of Holy Week to the *autos sacramentales*, the masterly spiritual plays of seventeenth-century Spain.

Von Balthasar's conclusion is not just that 'there need be nothing inevitable in the historical clash between Church and theatre' (*TD1*: 122) but also that the 'inner dramatic tension of revelation' and indeed 'all of today's influential theological trends . . . converge toward a theological dramatic theory yet without being able to reach it' (*TD1*: 125). His task, in the rest of the *Prolegomena*, is to establish a system of dramatic categories which will enable this theodramatic theory to be realized, reflecting initially upon the world as theatre, and human life as drama, before turning to the question of the role presented to us by human existence.

Von Balthasar begins with an exploration of 'The idea of the World Stage' (*TD1*: 135–257) recognizing that it is hardly an original idea. English speaking readers will be most familiar with it from Jacques' speech in Shakespeare's *As You Like It*, 'All the world's a stage . . . ', or from the inscription on the Globe Theatre (originating in John of Salisbury's *Policraticus*) that '*totus mundus agit histrionem*' (*TD1*: 162), but von Balthasar traces its origins back to the ancient world, to the philosophers and dramatists of classical Greece. He notes how glimpses of the metaphor are to be found in the biblical tradition (for example, the story of Job) and even in some of the Church Fathers, however hostile they might be to the theatre itself. But although he acknowledges the work of Shakespeare, for von Balthasar an 'ultimate clarity is attained at the level of the baroque world stage', and supremely in Caldéron's masterpiece, *The Great Theatre of the World*. Nevertheless this work remains 'held fast within the theatre metaphor' so that, even 'where the Christian dimension breaks through life's role-playing, the breakthrough itself is still described in the categories of the theatre' (*TD1*: 175).

With the emergence of Idealism (and post-Idealism) and the emphasis upon the knowing subject, von Balthasar sees the 'world theatre' metaphor dissolving within western drama. 'From now on the stage will be dominated by the sociologico-psychological drama on the one hand and the utopian-absurd drama on the other . . .' (*TD1*: 213). However this does at least offer him the opportunity to share some of the fruits of his literary studies, in the form of detailed excursuses on Grillparzer, Ibsen, Hofmannsthal, Shaw, and Pirandello among others. His conclusion is that, 'Through all its variations, in the ancient world, in Christianity, and in modern times, the "theatre of the world" rests on four leitmotifs which make it an arcane symbol of the dramatic dimension of existence . . .' (*TD1*: 249–50).

These four themes are themselves based on three distinctions: first, between 'the (temporal-spatial) finitude of the performed play and its non-finite meaning', that is the way the constraints of time and space encapsulated in the play (the classical 'three unities') mirror the finite reality of human existence and thus give meaning to it; second, between 'the "I" and the allotted role', namely how far the actor can identify with the role to be performed in order that it may become an authentic one; third, between 'the actor's responsibility for his performance and his responsibility to a director', which is to do with the freedom with which decisions can be made in the course of the drama; and all these lead to the fourth, which is the "dramatic tension' to which such distinctions give rise. The challenge then is to see how such perspectives go on to 'unpack' the dramatic categories which they imply, and it this task which he will undertake in the next chapter, 'Elements of the Dramatic' (*TD1*: 259–478).

So far von Balthasar is working 'on the basis of an understanding of the theatre that saw it as an illumination of existence'; in this next section he seeks to show how 'the theatre springs from existence and is characterised by it' (*TD1*: 259). So the first Dramatic Element is that the dramatic tension which arises during a performance 'must already be a part and parcel of existence. Existence itself must give rise to a "faith" that its tentative projects will somewhere meet with a "seeing", a "solution" that will satisfy' (*TD1*: 260). The drama should not be simply 'a poor imitation of life of life in the concrete with its unresolved problems'. 'Even when showing life "as it is", the drama must show how it ought to be and why it appears in such a way, or why things are not as they seem' (*TD1*: 262).

It follows then that the drama requires some creative input to illuminate human existence; in short it needs a play to perform. This leads von Balthasar to introduce the 'Three Elements of Dramatic Creativity' (*TD1*: 268–305). A play requires an 'author' to write the script, an 'actor' to perform it, and a 'director' to guide the performance. The author can only be God the Father who fashions the interplay of his characters out of his own creative experience. 'He must love his characters, but for that very reason he must also cherish their autonomy.' At the same time, there is a balance to be kept, 'if the author is to be "God the Father to his characters", he must not ultimately allow himself to be governed by their interplay' (*TD1*: 280). Then there is the actor through whom the *potential* of the drama is made *actual*. There are all kinds of issues which von Balthasar explores about what it means for an actor to take on a role and how far it can be identified with him or herself. But it is the actor's job 'to make himself entirely available, body and mind, for a fortuitous role and for the transitory pleasure of other human beings'. This in turn means that 'the actor exists on a knife's edge' and through his role 'presents society with possible models of freedom – embodied by him by way of anticipation' (*TD1*: 294–97). Finally there is needed a director to 'take responsibility for the play's performance', one who will 'mediate' between the author and actor upon whose creativity the play depends, in order to integrate their work into a dramatic whole.

However, this is not the end of the matter, for in addition to the writing of a play and directing of the rehearsals, there is also the performance of the drama. This involves a second triad of concepts, which von Balthasar calls 'the Three Elements of

Dramatic Realization' (*TD1*: 305–43). These involve the 'presentation', the 'audience' and the 'horizon' of meaning by which a play can come to be understood. For the drama to be realized, it has to be presented before an audience and, as the audience become engaged in the drama, the performance opens up a new horizon of meaning through which the audience can gain a fresh understanding of itself and its situation in the world. This is 'the twofold need to see and to surrender ourselves to something that transcends and gives meaning to the limited horizon of everyday life' (*TD1*: 308). It happens when the spectator, as part of the audience, 'is suddenly seized at a deeper level than he expected: he is no longer in charge of his own participation; he himself is called into question by his experience of the play; he is struck by "it"' (*TD1*: 315).

In von Balthasar's theodramatic theory, a trinitarian and soteriological dimension is introduced to this process, in which the Son as 'actor' places himself at the disposal of the Father, the 'author' of this saving drama, subject to the direction of the Holy Spirit. Thus 'Christian drama sets forth a horizon that, in virtue of its clarified idea of God, has a more unified effect than that of the ancient world, but at the same time its infinitely deepened dramatic context (embracing man and God) is patient of hidden and diverse interpretation'. In Christ the Son who enters the stage, the mind of God is revealed even as God the Father remains in the background as spectator; 'but since Father and Son are one, this role of spectator on God's part cannot be separated from his entering into the action on the stage. And when the Spirit proceeds from the Father and the Son and is breathed into the Church of Christ, something of God himself speaks in the mouth of the actors' (*TD1*: 319).

In contrast to this trinitarian drama, von Balthasar believes that all post-Christian drama can only point to a 'fragmenting' horizon. The last part of this section finds him looking in depth at two examples of where this can lead, first in the materialist determinism of Bertolt Brecht and then the absurdity of Eugène Ionesco. In both cases he finds there is ultimately a failure to set forth 'genuine persons in genuine, finite time' (*TD1*: 342) and this leads von Balthasar to set out the next Dramatic Element, namely 'Finitude', the finite constraints that human existence places upon the drama.

Von Balthasar addresses this element of constraint under three headings; namely Time, Situation and Death. In terms of time he maintains that there must, unlike in Brecht and Ionesco, be a meeting of 'horizontal' with 'vertical' time in that the drama of everyday existence must be viewed from the perspective of an eternal significance. This results in the 'paradox' of dramatic time. 'What is played is a unique event and yet as such it is a revelation of something timelessly valid, a metaphor, a parable' (*TD1*: 351). The same is true of situation and context. 'Dramatic action is possible and meaningful only within a given situation or constellation' (*TD1*: 353), yet this concrete setting somehow speaks to a universal understanding of human existence. The most graphic illustration of the finite constraints which underlie all dramatic action is the 'Theme of Death', a theme which von Balthasar explores, using a wide range of dramatic examples and under a number of headings, including 'Death as destiny', 'Death as the interpreter of Life', 'Death as atonement', 'Death and love', 'Death on behalf of someone else' and finally, 'The unmaking of kings', or as we might alternatively put it, 'Death as judgement'.

The final Element of the Dramatic is the 'Struggle for the Good'. For von Balthasar, 'Drama is concerned about change, whether it is change of man himself or of his environment' (*TD1*: 413). However, while the aim of human decision making is pursuit of 'the Good', this only reveals 'the questionable nature of the Good that can be attained on earth'. 'Every good for which man strives as a feasible possibility is surrounded, attacked and relativized by other goods and values' (*TD1*: 414). This leads von Balthasar into an extended discussion of the relationship between tragedy and comedy in light, not just of the Western dramatic tradition, but also of the Christian experience of faith, and indeed the story of Christ. An initial survey might suggest that tragedy deals with noble ideals while comedy addresses human foibles and fallibility, but von Balthasar's conclusion is different. 'It is not only in tragedy, but in comedy too that people act humanly, that is, responsibly, in all the vicissitudes of destiny. Otherwise the audience would not be interested' (*TD1*: 451).

The real question, he suggests, is not what category is to be used, but rather, 'How can the Good appear on stage if its ultimate criteria seem to be slipping away?' and 'How can the stage become (as it must) a place where a verdict is reached, a place of judgement?' These issues go beyond mere political or ethical comment; they lead into the matter of human judgment and personal responsibility. Here von Balthasar finishes with an extended excursus on the theme of 'Shakespeare and Forgiveness' (*TD1*: 465–78). He reflects on how in Shakespeare's earlier plays the emphasis is all on the mercy and grace that comes from human beings, whereas by the time of his final plays 'human forgiveness becomes so transparent, revealing the underlying quality of grace in of Being as such, that occasionally . . . thanksgiving takes over: there is nothing more to forgive' (*TD1*: 466). For von Balthasar, 'the dramatist causes the Good to predominate without feeling it necessary to reduce the totality of world events to some all-embracing formula'. Shakespeare 'takes up a position beyond tragedy and comedy, because the world he portrays is a mixture of both elements'. Similarly he 'rises above justice and mercy by allowing both of them to persist . . . But all the time he is utterly certain that the highest good is to be found in forgiveness' (*TD1*: 478).

In the final part of this opening volume, von Balthasar returns to one of the trends he picked up at the beginning, namely the relationship between 'role' and 'mission'. 'It is the question of *who*, in reality, plays the dramatic play of existence.' In turn this means that, 'The question that has to be asked is not "*What* kind of being is man?" but "Who am I?"' (*TD1*: 482). At this point von Balthasar returns to Greek philosophy and to the inscription on the portico of the Temple at Delphi: *Gnothi sauton*: Know thyself. He recognizes that there is a fundamental 'ambivalence' to this saying; it contains 'an admonition to man to consider God' and also to 'be aware of his human limitation' (*TD1*: 487). Moreover, as this saying was picked up and developed by later schools in the stoic and the neo-platonic traditions, von Balthasar sees that there are two different ways of exploring this theme: 'the stoics stress the individual's person emanation out of totality' and thus 'the rational performance of the limited role allotted to *me*' while the Neoplatonists 'put the emphasis on reflection upon the One', considering that 'the precondition for playing a good life is to keep an inner distance from what is being played and to keep in touch with universal Reason' (*TD1*: 491).

What von Balthasar does is to explore these two approaches, both in terms of their origins and in terms of later applications, under the headings 'Role as the Acceptance of Limitation' and 'Role as Alienation'. In 'Role as the Acceptance of Limitation' *(TD1*: 493–544), he explores how the theme of accepting human limitations has been picked up in modern psychology, particularly through the work of the three great founders of modern schools, namely Freud, Jung and Adler. His conclusion is that, 'Each in his own way, therefore, the great leaders of the three major schools of psychology will advocate that man should come to accept what he is; they will see the ultimate goal of therapy as that of integrating man into the totality that embraces him' (*TD1*: 505). A similar acceptance is found in sociology. 'By its very nature sociology is concerned, not with the question "Who am I?" (in contrast to everyone else), but with what is common to all human subjects, with their socialization' (*TD1*: 531). For von Balthasar what this whole approach is unable to do is 'to guarantee the personal uniqueness of individuals'. 'No doubt, the acceptance of limitation will have to be one element of human existence, but it cannot be an end in itself, nor can it be the key to the whole picture' (*TD1*: 544) – or should we say the whole play.

He then goes on to explore the second of the two approaches in 'Role as Alienation' (*TD1*: 545–89), taking as dialogue partners in this instance the resurgence of Idealism in the writings of Fichte, Schelling and Hegel. In both Fichte and Schelling, he finds that 'the question "Who am I?" is solved by saying: "I am who I make myself to be."' But for von Balthasar this answer 'does not fit into the totality of the construction of freedom, for, in order to be good, man would have to subordinate his own will entirely to the universal will . . . ' (*TD1*: 574). A similar problem is found in Hegel, who 'puts the nation, "the generalized individual", at the centre of his thought to which anything "particular" is a contrasting element' (*TD1*: 579) and which leads ultimately to the 'shattering of individuality' in his approach (*TD1*: 588). For von Balthasar it is clear that this is the path which leads to Marxism, 'where (quite logically) the individual is practically reduced to the level of material in the common cause . . . ' (*TD1*: 589).

Both these approaches have failed, in von Balthasar's opinion, 'because in each case the personal "I" has had to surrender itself to some all-embracing life or essence, and no necessary connection has been demonstrated between the life/essence and this particular "I"' (*TD1*: 591). In his next chapter, 'Attempts at Mediation' (*TD1*: 591–643), he examines four ways in which a bridge between the individual and the universal, so crucial to his understanding of dramatic role, has been attempted. In the ancient world there was the idea of the 'King' as representative of his people, a concept which came late – and not without controversy into the Bible, but whose usefulness von Balthasar considers now to have died out. There is also the idea of the individual or national 'Genius' but this is a notion too diffuse to be of much service. Von Balthasar then explores the concept of 'the Individual Law' found in the writings of the German philosopher Georg Simmel, only to conclude that his project 'suffers from an abstractness that prevents the interpersonal dimension from really expressing itself' (*TD1*: 624). In his view more hope is to be found in the last of these attempts, namely the 'Dialogue Principle' which emerged among a number of theologians at the beginning of the twentieth century. Von Balthasar notes both the Jewish and biblical origins of this rediscovery, particularly in the seminal work of Martin Buber, *Ich und Du*, (I and Thou) published in 1937. Buber's work emphasizes the revelation that takes place in the encounter, and where 'the "between" is not constituted by "I" and "thou" in separation but is always the prior place of encounter where both of them become for themselves for each other' (*TD1*: 634).

Von Balthasar recognizes a distinctive aspect of Buber's work in that God is 'not only the one who creates relationships but himself one pole of a relationship' (*TD1*: 635). However, he is wary of the way Buber focuses so clearly on the encounter and the 'I-thou' relationship, that less emphasis is given to how it leads to a discovery of 'vocation and mission' in the individual, although this is an element which von Balthasar detects being picked up by other theologians such as Franz Rosenzweig and Ferdinand Ebner. But for von Balthasar, it is this link between role and mission which is absolutely crucial, and also a pointer as to why it is necessary to pass from the Old Covenant into the New.

In *I and Thou* we also glimpse the world-fullness of the man who has been signed with a name. But only in Jesus Christ does it become clear how profoundly this definitive "I"- name signifies vocation, mission. In him, the "I" and the role become uniquely and ineffably one in the reality of his mission . . . (*TD1*: 645–6)

Von Balthasar now believes that an answer has been found to the question 'Who am I?' in terms of a role which is neither arbitrary nor imposed on human being. His critical insight is that what unites the concepts of role and identity is an understanding of 'mission' – and this is what is fulfilled in Christ. 'Once and for all the duality of "being" and "seeming", which goes through man's entire structure is absolutely overcome in the identity of person and mission in Christ' (*TD1*: 646). As he quotes from Theodor Haecker, 'Only in the drama of the God-Man do we find identity between the sublime actor and the role he has to play' (*TD1*: 646). But having established the possibility for a theodramatic understanding of role, it now remains to see who may appear in the cast, and it is this task which von Balthasar will undertake in his next two volumes.

4.2 *DRAMATIS PERSONAE: MAN IN GOD*

Following on from his initial exploration of dramatic categories, von Balthasar sets out the approach his theological dramatic theory will take.

Our aim is to present the same fundamental themes – God and the creature, the structure and situation of the world and man, the Mediator and his presence (the Church and all that is associated with her) and the movement of history – in three stages. The first stage is the *point of departure* (the "dramatis personae", as it were); the second is the *course of the action*; and the third is the *final play*. (*TD2*: 11)

(And in light of our earlier chapter looking at some of the 'Key Influences' on his work, perhaps we should not be surprised to note how these 'fundamental themes' resonate with those major themes which von Balthasar identified in Barth as ones which Catholic theology would have to take seriously in future, namely the foundations for christocentrism, for the historicity of nature, and the created character of worldly truth (*KB*: 383).)

The first stage, the *Dramatis Personae*, is dealt with in the next two volumes of the *Theo-Drama*. However, von Balthasar recognizes that there are two issues which he has to address first before his list of dramatic characters can be properly understood. The first is a general one; in order for any list of characters to be meaningful for an audience, it needs to know the kind of role and the kind of drama in which they are involved. The second is a specifically theological one, which is the issue of how human beings can play a part in this divine drama which starts and ends with God; or as von Balthasar states it very boldly; 'who else acts, who else *can* act, if God is on the stage? . . . Where is there any room for man's "something", if God, by nature, must be "everything" (Sir. 43:27) if he is to be God at all?' (*TD2*: 17–18).

It is these questions that von Balthasar addresses in the first part, 'The Approach' (*TD2*: 17–169). He wants 'to establish the standpoint of the "characters"', to explore what options will be open to them in this drama, and he does this in his characteristically comprehensive way in four sub-sections.

> First we shall let the phenomenon speak for itself (A); then we shall attempt a purely intramundane presentation of the drama of existence (B); the ultimate failure of this attempt will legitimately point us toward a transcendent, theological drama (C), which has the power to interpret and expound itself (D). (*TD2*:19)

Von Balthasar is conscious that the *Theo-Drama* is a following on from his *Aesthetics*, and so notes that 'it is important to reflect on the way "aesthetics" opens up to and moves across into "dramatics", even in the realm of intramundane phenomena'. This is true of worldly beauty as it is of the divine glory, and so in interpreting itself, we return to some of the key terms found before in *The Glory of the Lord*, namely 'Form', 'Word' and 'Election'. 'The beautiful form presents itself to us, it "attests" itself, its character exhibits grace, favour (*Huld*)' (*TD2*: 23). This evokes a response, 'the interplay of grace and gratitude: a dialogue' for, 'Where there is dialogue, there must be *word*' (*TD2*: 24). Moreover, the 'form and the word within it awaken and summon us; they awaken our *freedom* and bid us attend to the call that comes to us from the form' (*TD2*: 28–9). This sense of being struck or touched is in turn an "election", and in terms of the drama, 'no one is enraptured without returning from this encounter with a personal mission'. 'The third element is latent in the first and second: God only shows himself to someone, only enraptures him, in order to commission him' (*TD2*: 31).

In the next chapter, 'The Unfinished Drama', von Balthasar addresses the question: 'what kind of relationship must there be between the world and the Absolute, between man and God, if the levelling produced by transitoriness and death is not to cripple the dramatic dimension of existence from within?' The answer is to be found in 'an idea of God which allowed him to take part – an inner, divine, absolute part – in the drama of mortal existence without threatening his absolute nature'. It is such an idea that 'provides a link between early, *mythic* thought and Christian faith'. 'Christianity alone provides a new approach: God has become man without ceasing to be God' (*TD2*: 45). This does not involve any diminution of the human drama. 'The tragic dimension of personal existence is not softened: in fact it is wrenched to its very limit: in the Cross' (*TD2*: 49). This leads von Balthasar to assert that 'in Christian terms, the dramatic dimension of human existence can only be taken in complete seriousness – and that accordingly, the Christian revelation can only appear in its full stature – if it is presented as being dramatic *at its very core*' (*TD2*: 51).

In turn this leads von Balthasar to set out the characteristics of theo-drama in 'The Unfolding Drama'. His first point is that since 'God has made his own the tragic situation of human existence' there can be 'No External Standpoint' (*TD2*: 54). 'In this play all the spectators must eventually become fellow actors, whether they wish to or not' (*TD2*: 58). It also means that the old distinctions between 'lyrical' and 'epic' approaches in theology are overcome in the new approach which challenges the believer to be a 'witness' to the drama. 'We shall not get beyond the alternatives of "lyrical" and "epic", spirituality (prayer and personal involvement) and theology (the objective discussion of facts), so long as we fail to include the dramatic dimension of revelation in which alone they can discover their unity' (*TD2*: 57). It then leads him in 'Convergence toward Theo-Drama' (*TD2*: 62–77) to pick up the nine trends of modern theology identified in his *Prolegomena*. It is a *'play of freedoms'* which takes seriously the 'horizontal history of the individual and mankind' but at the same time allows for the 'event' in which 'aspects of the end-time and eternity break in'. It sees 'no opposition between Church structure and Christian orthopraxy' (any more than between authority and discipleship in the calling of the Twelve). It engages with the 'political' in its commitment to be salt and leaven in the kingdom, to the 'dialogic' as Jesus shares in conversation and through parables, and to the 'futuristic' as the Spirit leads believers into all truth.

Having thus demonstrated that 'the substantial efforts of modern theology are concentric, converging on a theo-drama', and that, 'divorced from this centre they largely cancel each other out' (*TD2*: 77), von Balthasar then asks whether all these themes can be held together in a 'Single Drama', and whether the 'once-for-all drama of Christ' can 'be exalted as the norm of the entire dramatic dimension of human life'. This would require two things to happen simultaneously: 'the abyss of all tragedy must be plumbed to the bottom (which no purely human tragedy can do); and, in it, and transcending it, we must discern the element of gracious destiny that genuinely touches human existence (and not merely *seems* to touch it.)' (*TD2*: 84). It is this double requirement which von Balthasar sees as being achieved in the story of Jesus' birth, death and resurrection. 'As the perfect man with his peerless drama, he is the living framework within which every human destiny is acted out; every human destiny is judged by his perfection and saved by his redeeming meaning' (*TD2*: 87).

This 'Convergence toward Theo-Drama' in turn requires a 'Theodramatic Hermeneutics' to interpret it. Von Balthasar maintains that 'in revealing himself in Jesus Christ, God interprets himself – and this must involve his giving an interpretation, in broad outline and in detail, of his plan for the world . . .'. However such an interpretation must also involve some human co-operation.

> For God does not play the world drama all on his own; he makes room for man to join in the acting. In other words: when God, acting in Jesus Christ, utters, expresses himself, his language must be intelligible to the world, or at least *become* intelligible through the divine Spirit, who teaches

men's hearts to listen and to speak so that they can utter a word in reply. (*TD2*: 91)

So in this chapter von Balthasar identifies the key features required for such a hermeneutics. They include: acknowledgement of the 'Church's teaching office', not simply as a timeless repository of truth but as a participant in the drama to witness that 'the event that has taken place between God and man is to be proclaimed to the world as something that is *always taking place in an ever new "now"*' (*TD2*: 102); recognition that the testimony of Scripture is not external to the events but also has a role to play in the drama as 'a Word that journeys with us' (*TD2*: 102) and 'a Word that is both attested and generative' (*TD2*: 106); 'the principle of the "ever-greater" which applies to all that concerns God and his revelation' (and which is based ultimately on von Balthasar's understanding of the *analogia entis*) (*TD2*: 128); and finally the 'Freedom of Faith' in response to the divine revelation (*TD2*: 130–6). The chapter closes with two Excursuses, the first dealing with 'Approaches adopted by early Christian Apologists' and the second looking at Irenaeus' very distinctive account of how 'Truth vindicates itself' in his *Adversus Haereses* (*Against Heresies*).

In the final chapter of this section, headed the 'Themes of Dramatic Theology', von Balthasar offers an overview of some biblical themes which offer a genuinely dramatic element to the unfolding of God's revelation. He begins with the idea of 'God's Lawsuit', found both in the prophets and in the letters of Paul. He even goes on to imagine what this might mean for 'the Total Drama as Lawsuit', borrowing Markus Barth's synopsis of how this might be set out as a five act play: the first, 'the court of judgment of God's wrath'; the second as 'God sends his Son as the Advocate'; the third, 'the Resurrection of Jesus from the dead'; the fourth, 'the sending and work of the Spirit' leading to the fifth, 'the visible manifestation of salvation – in the form of the Last Judgement' (*TD2*: 155–9). Other themes are 'Christ's Dramatic Struggle' (reflecting on Gustaf Aulén's account of the atonement in *Christus Victor*) and the 'Drama of Discipleship', which is explored variously in the Gospels, the writings of the Fathers, even down to the Ignatian Exercises, and the purpose of which is to show that 'the sense of the drama of a life lived in discipleship of Christ has remained alive down the centuries, even if it was excessively isolated from the manuals of dogmatics' (*TD2*: 168).

Having mapped his 'Approach' von Balthasar is now in a position to outline the characters. Interestingly, he first addresses the question of 'the Stage'. He quotes from Genesis 1.1, 'In the beginning God created the heavens and the earth'. This is significant for two reasons. In the first place it means that this stage 'is not a neutral area'; it 'has been designed for the *one* drama that is to be played on it' and is 'determined in part by the action that is to take place there' (*TD2*: 173). It also means that 'heaven and earth have been created as distinct realms with a view to a drama in which each pole has its own, proper, positive role to play' (*TD2*: 187). It is not simply the case that, as with Shakespeare, 'All the world's a stage', but that in this theo-drama the stage must include both the heavens and the earth.

But having sketched the area for this dramatic engagement, von Balthasar has still to deal with the fundamental question he raised at the beginning, namely who can act if God is on the stage? This raises the crucial issue of freedom, in terms of the relationship between the infinite and unlimited freedom of the Creator and the finite and limited freedom of the creature. It is this which he addresses in his next section, 'Infinite and Finite Freedom' (*TD2*: 189–334). 'Theo-drama (as distinct from merely human drama) is only possible where "God", or "a God", or some accredited representative of God, steps onto the stage of life's play as "a person" in the action, separate from the other characters' (*TD2*: 189). But to be able to act in this way, God must also have a 'sovereign ability' out of his own freedom 'to create and send forth finite but genuinely free beings . . . in such a way that, without vitiating the infinite nature of God's freedom, a genuine opposition of freedoms can come about' (*TD2*: 190). It is this 'opposition of freedoms' which allows for a genuine drama to take place. It also means that in von Balthasar's view 'we have no alternative but to start on the basis of the interrelationship between the two freedoms' since 'we cannot illuminate the structure of finite freedom without the light that radiates from Christ and falls on the divine freedom' (*TD2*: 206).

Von Balthasar begins then with 'Finite Freedom'. There are two 'poles' or 'pillars' to this freedom, the first that sense of 'self-possession' or 'being present to myself' by which I know that I exist, and the second which is that awareness of other beings which are different to me, and indeed which leaves me open to the reality of Being itself. The two things go together. 'The one identical experience of being discloses two things simultaneously: the utter incommunicability (or uniqueness) and the equally total communicability of being . . . I am unique, but only by making room for countless others to be unique' (*TD2*: 209). In terms of the first pole, finite freedom has been identified with 'Autonomous Motion', with the ability to be and to decide for oneself, a freedom from external compulsions or constraints. However, von Balthasar goes on to explore another understanding of freedom linked with the second pole, namely freedom as 'Consent'. This is an approach to freedom particularly linked with Augustine, whose 'starting point is not the definition of finite freedom as freedom to choose good or evil' but rather the understanding that 'finite freedom, which is necessarily equipped with this ability can only fulfil itself within the context of infinite freedom' (*TD2*: 232). We might characterize this understanding as an emphasis on freedom not *from* external constraints but rather *for* that which it was created. For von Balthasar adopting this approach means that

> we begin to see that finite freedom as *autexousion*, as consent to oneself in the freedom of self-possession, is by no means alienated but rather inwardly fulfilled by consenting to that Being-in-its-totality which has now revealed itself as that which freely grounds all things, as that which, in infinite freedom, creates finite freedom. (*TD2*: 242)

Von Balthasar then turns to address 'Infinite Freedom'. He is concerned in the first place to demonstrate that the act of creation does not diminish God's infinite freedom. 'It becomes more and more apparent that creation in no way sets limits to the divine freedom . . . . ' Instead 'the world as a totality, its being and its existence, is dependent on the infinite freedom in which God desires to create in the first place and then actually does create' (*TD2*: 244–5). The same is true for the relationships and workings of the Trinity. 'God is not only by nature free in his self-possession, in his ability to do what he will with himself; for that very reason he is also free to do what he will with his own nature. That is, he can surrender himself; as Father, he can share the same Godhead with the Son, and, as Father and Son, he can share the same Godhead with the Spirit' (*TD2*: 256). It is this freedom to let go, to surrender in love which gives time and space for the Theo-Drama to take place. It also becomes clear 'why finite freedom can really fulfil itself in infinite freedom and in no other way . . . It can only be what it is, that is an image of infinite freedom, imbued with a freedom of its own, by getting in tune with the (trinitarian) "law" of absolute freedom (of self-surrender) . . . ' (*TD2*: 259).

From this a number of things follow. There is no point speculating about other possible worlds since 'there is nothing hindering us from extolling the world God actually chose as the best, *because* it has been chosen by God, in his absolute freedom, as the adequately clear embodiment of the "idea" of the freely obedient Son' (*TD2*: 269). The role of finite freedom is preserved because the 'personal "idea" of each individual finite freedom lies in the incarnate Son in such a way that each is given a unique participation on the Son's uniqueness' (*TD2*: 270). This is reflected in the relative openness of God's plan, which 'has "time" and "space" for all the created times and spaces in which this plan is able to realise itself in the context of the world' (*TD2*: 279). It is also why von Balthasar is wary of speaking of 'God's immutability', 'precisely because it is essential to keep before us his absolute freedom, manifested in his plan for the world as a freedom to purse his (trinitarian) freedom' (*TD2*: 280). The rest of this sub-section is a consideration how this freedom 'accompanies' and is 'accepted' in human being, the role of prayer and praise in response to such freedom, and then a final reflection on 'grace'.

It is significant that it closes with an excursus on the theme of the 'Image and Likeness of God' in light of Genesis 1.26ff, for this is a passage which was central to Karl Barth's anthropology. Yet in his treatment, von Balthasar argues that it requires the 'analogy of being' to interpret it properly. This same theme will become very clear in the final chapter of this section in which von Balthasar offers his own anthropology under the heading, 'Man'. He begins by acknowledging that the previous section on freedom comes as a kind of "Prologue in Heaven" but asserts that this is important because 'if we want to ask about man's "essence", we can only do so in the midst of his dramatic perform-ance of existence. There is no other anthropology but the dramatic' (*TD2*: 335). This means that 'he can and must define *himself*. Yet, as we have seen, he cannot step out of the dramatic action in which he finds himself in order to reflect on which part he will play. He is part of the play without being asked, and he in fact plays a role' (*TD2*: 341).

Von Balthasar next addresses the 'pre-Christian' understand-ing of 'Man and Nature'. This he believes is characterized by a series of tensions, (or 'polarities' to use the term he borrows from Przywara). 'Man' is 'rooted in the Cosmos' (*TD2*: 346ff) but this includes both the visible cosmos of which he is essentially a part and also the divine cosmos which is not directly visible. Man is also 'Spirit and Body' (*TD2*: 355ff), 'Man and Woman' (*TD2*: 365ff) and 'Individual and Community' *(TD2*: 382ff). These polarities provide a tension, a riddle to existence that is not cap-able of being resolved in simply human terms. 'In all three dimensions, man seems to be built according to a polarity, obliged to engage in reciprocity, always seeking complementarity and peace in the other pole.' And in the unresolved tension between these poles, humanity is threatened by the ultimate reminder of finitude. 'He is always found crossing the boundary, and thus he is defined most exactly by that boundary with which death brutally confronts him . . . ' (*TD2*: 355).

However, this 'pre-Christian' understanding is radically chal-lenged by the 'New Christian Reality' (*TD2*: 394–416). Initially the appearance of Christ serves to 'heighten the tensions' which have been outlined before, just as within the framework of the 'analogy of being' the 'greater dissimilarity' between Creator and creature becomes ever clearer. However, precisely in this crisis, 'Jesus Christ is the proof that the supernatural "heightening of tension" in man . . . does not inhumanly tear his existence apart. Jesus Christ proves that existence in this tension is liveable' (*TD2*: 406). What Christ offers is 'the gift of a sharing in God's nature' so that 'the individual who receives the word acquires a new qual-ity: he becomes a *unique person*' (*TD2*: 402). This leads to a 'New Rhythm' in human life (and here the ecclesial consequences of von Balthasar's theology become increasingly evident). There is a new relationship between body and spirit as the believer is incorporated into the 'bodily life of the Church'; a new 'suprasexual (and not sexless) relationship', after the model of Christ and his Church, becomes available to men and women so that sex 'need no longer be the exclusive model of human fruitfulness'; and the relationship between individual and community is transcended by participation in the *communio sanctorum*, the fellowship of the saints (*TD2*: 411–16).

Von Balthasar then briefly addresses some 'post-Christian' approaches to anthropology in terms of the ongoing influence of Gnosticism and the emergence of what he calls modern-day 'Titanisms', in which humanity itself lays claim to divinity (as in Feuerbach and Nietzsche), before summarizing what has been achieved in this volume. 'We have presented the main characters of the theo-drama: God and man.' Moreover, from this presentation two key things have emerged. First that 'God is not simply the "Other" (the "partner"); he is so high above all created things that he is just as much the "non-Other" '(which means that 'man' can not be inferred or deduced from God). But at the same time, 'God has given him a genuine, spiritual freedom which, because it has been really *given*, cannot be "upstaged" by God's infinite freedom but has to fulfil itself in its proper area (in God, where else?). The primal drama is played between divine and human freedom' (*TD2*:428). This drama requires a third actor, the 'Mediator between God and man' and it is he who is the subject of the next volume.

4.3 *DRAMATIS PERSONAE: PERSONS IN CHRIST*

If in Volume II von Balthasar was establishing the preconditions for human participation in the divine drama, then Volume III is where the roles are made clear, as *Man in God* is followed by *Persons in Christ*. Moreover, given that God in Christ is to be the principal actor in this drama, we should not be surprised to find that the focus on a theo-dramatic anthropology in the previous volume is here followed by a more extensive concentration upon Christology. Yet in focusing on Christ who is the 'consummating protagonist of the entire drama', von Balthasar does not want to infer that 'the final act of the drama has been acted out in advance' or that 'the relationship between God and creation has been stripped of all drama'. Rather we need to see how Christ 'expands the acting area, rather than narrows it'; how he

> simultaneously opens up the greatest possible intimacy and the greatest possible distance . . . between God and man' and so 'does not decide the course of the play in advance but gives man an otherwise unheard-of freedom to decide for or against the God who has so committed himself. (*TD3*: 20–1)

Von Balthasar begins with some qualifying comments. In the 'Impact of the Meteor' he acknowledges that while the coming of Christ has had an overwhelming impact on world history, it is not something to be measured simply in phenomenological or historical terms. He reflects on the implications of the 'Dramatic Aspect of Inclusion in Christ' to show how 'in Christ, God opens up that personal sphere of freedom within which the particular (individual or collective) characters are given their ultimate human face, their mission or "role"; it is left up to them to play their part well or ill' (*TD3*: 38). Then, in the 'Acting Area' von Balthasar reminds us that it is no 'empty' stage upon which Christ appears, but rather one which he has helped to create, and whose space forms around the '*three fundamental articulations of his existence*' (*TD3*: 43), namely the 'Kingdom', the 'Cross' and the 'Resurrection' so that in Christ, the 'empty area between finite and infinite becomes a place "inhabited" by God . . .' (*TD3*: 54).

Following these qualifications, von Balthasar maps out the task ahead, which is to 'sketch a Christology that will ultimately lead into the doctrine (here presupposed) according to which all the characters (and their actions) relevant to the theo-drama are "included" in Christ' (*TD3*: 55). The first task then is 'to gain access to the figure of Christ' and the second 'to proceed to a speculative Christology and raise the question of the meaning and limitations of the "Chalcedonian model"'. But this is only possible by means of an investigation, not just of the New Testament sources but also the results of modern biblical scholarship, a task which he undertakes in his next extensive sub-section, 'The Problem of Method' (*TD3*: 59–148). His study takes account of the 'Impact of Historico-critical Neutrality', the 'Hiatus between *Historie* and *Geschichte*' and the significance of Bultmann and Form criticism. His analysis of this scholarship leads him to the conclusion that there is what he terms a 'Continuity in Discontinuity' (*TD3*: 78ff); that far from being 'projected onto' an earlier historical Jesus, the development of christological titles in the New Testament is itself 'rooted' in the experience of the first Christians and the early Church from the very beginning; and that

> within the very framework of the form-critical method itself, which is always looking for the *Sitz im Leben* in the community, we find evidence of a continuity (in the discontinuity) different from that of the attempts of the post-Bultmannites . . . for example, the attention given to Jesus' claim to full authority, containing as it does an 'implicit Christology'. (*TD3*: 86)

For von Balthasar, the crucial question then becomes 'How did Jesus understand his mission within the span of life allotted to him?' which in turn raises the problems associated with apocalyptic, namely Jesus' self-consciousness and the Cross. He maintains that there are 'two poles to the life and consciousness of Jesus: on the one hand, he expects the imminent arrival of the kingdom, but, on the other hand, he does so in the calm security of someone who lives his life entirely for his mission' (*TD3*: 92). Then, as he seeks to explain the dogmatic 'overlay' by which the early Church imposed christological titles so soon after the events of his death, von Balthasar goes on to suggest; 'Might not Jesus' consciousness of his mission have been that he had to abolish the world's estrangement from God in its entirety – that is to the very end – or, in Pauline and Johannine terms, deal with the sin of the whole world? In that case *after* his earthly mission the decisively and (humanly speaking) immeasurable part was still to come' (*TD3*: 110). This means that Jesus' life cannot be interpreted along 'wisdom' lines but must follow an 'apocalyptic' rhythm, as he prepares for his 'hour' which is to come.

For von Balthasar, this also raises the topic of 'representation', or 'mankind's incorporation into Christ', so that what is undertaken by Jesus becomes effective in his disciples and the life of the world. This is not merely a christological but also a theodramatic issue, since it is about how far Christ can be said to 'include' humanity in his theodramatic role. Von Balthasar explores four ways in which this issue can be addressed under the heading, the 'Theme Transposed': first in terms of Jesus' 'hour' and its impact upon his disciples; second in terms of whether the post-Easter community is called to live in this same 'hour'; third in terms of how Jesus is to be portrayed (as he was or as he is?); and fourth, since Jesus is transcendent and 'cannot be held fast by the laws of temporal historiography', how far will his figure be 'clearly legible' amidst the plurality of interpretations that will emerge? (*TD3*: 122). His conclusion, after further examination, is that the 'four areas exhibit an inner dynamism – both in the Christ-event itself and in its intertwining with the faith of the disciples and of the primitive Church – that highlights a wealth of dramatic elements' (*TD3*: 148).

This examination of method leads onto von Balthasar's consideration of Christology, under the heading 'Christ's Mission and Person'. His starting point is that of 'Mission as a Basic Concept' because the assumption that 'Jesus possessed a sense of mission that was eschatological and universal' has proved to be the only way to balance the various exegetical and dogmatic issues which arose in the previous discussions (*TD3*: 149). Moreover, he also finds it to be integral to the Gospels; 'the idea of mission, which is at the centre of John's Christology and expresses both the trinitarian and the soteriological dimensions of the mind of Jesus, is also most definitely present in the Synoptics . . . ' (*TD3*: 151). In the story of Jesus, and supremely in his baptism, we see 'identity being given along with mission' and this is found too in 'the abstract conciliar formulas of Nicea and Chalcedon'. 'The whole person of the Son is involved in his work for the world, and his whole human nature, in all its phases and aspects, ministers to it. It is for this work that the Son has been sent' (*TD3*: 157).

The next topic to be covered is 'Jesus' consciousness of Mission', a topic which in light of Paul's concentration on the Cross and Resurrection, von Balthasar regards as inescapable. However, it also raises a number of connected issues, among them the relationship between Jesus' human and divine consciousness, and the question as to when he first became aware of his mission, and thus his identity. In terms of the first issue, von Balthasar's response is that,

If . . . we take Jesus' entire awareness that he belongs to God and refer it to his mission, we shall not need to agonise over the relation of his human self-consciousness to his divine self-consciousness. The task given him by the Father, that is, that of expressing God's Fatherhood though his entire being, through his life and death in and for the world, totally occupies his self-consciousness and fills it to the very brim. (*TD3*: 172)

As regards the second, for von Balthasar this is where 'the assertion that *Mariology* is an inner component of Christology shows its relevance' as the themes of the Annunciation show how Jesus' consciousness of mission could be inculcated from childhood (*TD3*: 175). Moreover, this is a consciousness which, in human terms, develops over time and into history. 'Jesus undergoes an historical learning process with regard to his fellow men and their tradition, but essentially this is paralleled by an inward learning whereby he is *initiated more and more deeply* into the meaning and scope of his mission' (*TD3*: 179).

Such a mission-based Christology also has trinitarian implications, for 'at the point of distinction between the Father's purpose and the Son's obedience, we discern an essential poise, an essential communication between Father and Son which can only be the operation of the Holy Spirit' (*TD3*: 183). For von Balthasar 'the Spirit has a two-fold face from all eternity;' as the One 'breathed forth from the one love of Father and Son' the Spirit is both 'the expression of their united freedom' and also 'the objective witness to their difference-in-unity or unity-in-difference' (*TD3*: 187). This leads him to introduce what he terms the "Trinitarian Inversion", whereby the Spirit who is breathed forth from the Father during the time of the Son's incarnation, in his *status exinanitionis* or time of self-emptying, becomes the Spirit who is breathed forth by the Son into his Church and the world during the time of his ascension or *status exaltationis* (*TD3*: 189), thus offering a trinitarian framework to account for the so-called 'two-stage Christology' evidenced in the New Testament documents.

Von Balthasar helpfully summarizes what has been achieved, namely 'that the Christology of consciousness here outlined, taking "mission" as our guide, provides the basis for the development of a theodramatic theory in several respects', of which three are most important: the first is that 'in the identity of Jesus' person and mission, we have the realization par excellence of what is meant by a dramatic "character": namely a figure who, by carrying out his role, either attains his true face or . . . unveils his hidden face'; the second that 'it is the identity of character and mission that really makes the world drama into a theo-drama' and the third that 'in his person and mission, Christ is the "last Adam", the one who gives meaning to the whole play; as such he embodies mankind's whole dramatic situation in its relationship to itself and to God' (*TD3*: 201).

Von Balthasar has not quite finished his exploration of Christology. There follows a further examination of the 'theo-logical concept of Person' (in which he notes among other things that the language of *prosopon* and *persona* involve terms which were initially borrowed from the stage) and also of the role of the 'Analogia Entis in Christology' (which reflects the continuing influence of his erstwhile mentor Erich Przywara). But the final part of this section, entitled 'Inclusion in Christ', points to where his argument is leading. Von Balthasar's conclusion is that 'it is not only the Logos but Christ who is the *mediator of creation*' which in turn means that 'all things could only be created with a view to their being perfected in the second Adam – something that only comes to light in the being and consciousness of the Son as he carried out his mission of bringing everything to per-fection'. It is this 'normative archetypal quality' that determines Christ's crucial role in the theo-drama. 'In the role of God, Jesus Christ is his valid exposition and presence in the world' but at the same time 'the role played by Jesus Christ yields the principle for allotting roles to all the other actors' and so 'it is from this center that human conscious subjects are allotted personalizing roles or missions (charisms)' (*TD3*: 257–8).

Von Balthasar's argument is that it is in the identity between person and mission in Christ that we find the most perfect real-ization of what it means to be a dramatic character, as Christ fulfils his role in free obedience to his Father's sending. But it also points to the way in which other characters can discover their part and play their role as fully human beings. For von Balthasar's argument is that it is only in Christ that human beings can become real persons and act as theo-dramatic char-acters in their own right. And the rest of this volume will seek to offer just such a christological basis for the whole of creation to play its part in the drama, under the heading of 'Theological Persons' (*TD3*: 263–461).

In 'Chosen and Sent Forth', von Balthasar reminds us that while, in 'the acting area opened up by Christ, created conscious subjects can become persons of theological relevance, co-actors in theo-drama' (*TD3*: 263), they remains different to him. They may have been 'chosen in Christ' but the one who calls and invites them to respond is God. There is the possibility that such a vocation may be refused and 'if the free acceptance of vocation and mission involves our acquiring theological personhood, it follows that its refusal may profoundly threaten the person' (*TD:* 266). It involves a process of self-discovery as 'we discover God by obeying him, our fellow men by serving them, and ourselves, whom we only encounter in such service and obedience' (*TD3*: 271). And it is one which involves people not just as individuals, but as social beings, as persons in community, the essentially ecclesial dimensions of which he will draw out next in 'Woman's Answer' and 'The Church of Jews and Gentiles'.

If von Balthasar's theodramatic perspective is distinctive and original, his approach to Mary and the Church is much more traditional and Catholic. He starts where he left off in the previous volume, with that 'fundamental feature of human nature: the polarity of man and woman' (*TD3*: 283). This leads him to explore the role of woman as 'essentially an answer (*Ant-Wort*)' to man, as his helper and home provider, 'the vessel of fulfilment designed for him', although she is also 'equipped with her own explicit fruitfulness' (*TD3*: 284–5). While the origins of this approach can clearly be found in the Genesis story of Adam and Eve, this is not a reading which will commend itself to all contemporary Christians. However, this aspect of feminine response and receptivity leads von Balthasar to see 'an analogy for the relationship between God and the creature'. In turn, 'Once the intramundane (man-woman) aspect and the supramundane (God-world) aspect come together in Jesus Christ, we can begin to see what woman's christological position might be' (*TD3*: 287–8). For in Jesus Christ we have not just a divine Person but also a man, and this means that we are not just dealing with any woman, but in particular with Mary, the mother of Christ.

This leads von Balthasar into an extended discussion of Mary in terms both of Christology and ecclesiology. He has a particular interest in exploring how these issues can be worked out in light of the theological developments which led to the Vatican statements on Mariology, namely her Immaculate Conception (1854) and Bodily Assumption into heaven (1950). But more importantly for our purposes is the way Mary is developed both as a theodramatic character in her own right and as one who has a special role in the Church. For von Balthasar, 'Mary is a dramatic character because her existence lies between the various states of human nature' (*TD3*: 318). Her life with Christ stands on both sides of the Easter event and her involvement with the Church points to the age to come. Thus she has a

> two-fold mission; as a Mother, she has to mediate – in the requisite purity – everything that her Child needs; as her Son's "companion" and "bride", she must be able to share his sufferings in a way appropriate to her, and what most fits her for this task is her utter purity, which means that she is profoundly exposed and vulnerable. (*TD3*: 323)

At the same time, by virtue of her unique relationship to Christ, Mary also has a role in bringing to birth and shaping the Church. Here von Balthasar recognizes that the relationship of sexual complementarity, however important, is insufficient to reduce everything to a single 'Marian formal principle'; even the extent to which she can be regarded as a 'type' of the Church must allow for a multiplicity of meanings. 'It can mean that 'Mary, as Mother of Christ, is the "fleshly" model of the Church (the Church gives birth to Christ "spiritually")' or 'that she is more: namely the individual, real and comprehensive model for all believers' or finally 'that she is the fearless prototype of the Church and, as such, the Church's eschatological goal' and thus 'the personal epitome of the Church of the New Testament' (*TD3*: 338–9). To explore this in more detail, von Balthasar takes his 'Christology of mission' further to see how it might serve to shape a Marian perspective of Church. His starting point is to see the Church's personality as 'the interplay [*perichoresis*] of personal and social missions . . . around the center, which is the mission of Mary' (*TD3*: 353).

What renders the 'bridal' and 'maternal' Church fruitful in this context is the creation of the Church as an 'institution', which so far from denying the 'nuptial' event, 'actually makes it possible for this event to be a here and now reality at every point though history'. Moreover, this relationship is characterized by five aspects which in turn give a shape to the Church as institution; namely that she must have 'a bodily constitution . . . matching the inner, pneumatic vitality infused into her', that 'the event in which the Church is "born" from Christ is a continual event happening in the here and now', that there must be 'an objectified love and holiness within the Church', that there will be a 'new form of service' both in terms of official and unofficial ministries within her life, and finally that there will be an ongoing 'tension between the "episcopal" and "prophetic" office', both of which are needed to preserve the Church's life and faith (*TD3*: 353–8).

At this last point we might discern a faint resonance with the difficulties that von Balthasar himself experienced in his relationship with the authorities of his own order when leaving the Jesuits. But his final position remains unmistakeably Catholic.

> Only the Catholic Church has this bipolar character of Marian, subjective holiness and Petrine objective holiness. It constitutes her irreducible, inner dramatic tension and is what makes her the extension ("fullness", "body") of Christ as well as his partner ("Bride") enabling her to participate in Christ's redemptive mission and, undergirding this, in his trinitarian being. (*TD3*: 358)

All of this is not to say that Mary and the Church are the only creaturely characters in the *Theo-Drama*. Reflection on what it means to be the 'Church of Jews and Gentiles' will include attending to the role of 'Israel' (*TD3*: 371–401), as the community blessed by God's original covenant with Abraham, as well as the 'Nations', (*TD3*: 401–21) those who stand outside that original covenant, just as there are many who similarly remain outside the covenant of grace mediated through Jesus Christ. Von Balthasar takes a very similar line to Barth as regards the challenge posed to Christianity by the continuance of Israel, namely that this is a mystery not to be resolved nor revealed before the end. At the same time, his firmly christological and Marian ecclesiology leads him decisively to reject that approach to the challenge of other religions which he believes to be characterized by Karl Rahner's notion of 'anonymous Christianity'.

Von Balthasar has not quite finished with ecclesiology, although he recognizes that most of what is needed has already been spoken in 'Mary's Answer'. In the 'Church as Union' he reminds us of the 'mystery' of the Church as 'the genuine inter-personal community', a union which is both 'shakeable' (since founded on Christ) and 'precarious' (because composed of sinners (*TD3*: 428)). It is sustained by 'sacrament', which mediates 'not the Church but Christ's self-dedication to the Church, so that the individual may be drawn into the Church's mission' (*TD3*: 430) and is 'transcendent' because the Church exists not for herself but for the entire world (*TD3*: 435). Sadly, the Church is also divided, and here von Balthasar is absolutely at one with Barth's verdict on the scandal of division, 'We should treat it as we treat our sins and those of others' (*TD3*: 446).

Given the emphasis which von Balthasar has placed on the Church as a theodramatic character, we should not be surprised to discover that his chapter dealing with the 'Individual' (*TD3*: 447–61) is a much shorter one. He does briefly explore the roles of 'discipleship' and 'witness' but primarily within the context of the Christian community. His treatment of 'The Individual in the World', though, is noticeably brief and less specific. What is perhaps more surprising is the much greater attention which he gives to the roles of 'Angels and Demons' (*TD3*: 465–501); although in this matter he is not simply respecting the place which these occupy in the Biblical witness but also engaging with some of the very distinctive views which Karl Barth has expressed on the subject.

However, this third volume ends with a reminder that all these characters have their role to play only because of that divine drama which begins within the persons and relationships of the Trinity. Von Balthasar closes this volume by reflecting on what his theodramatic theory means for traditional understandings of the 'economic' and the 'absolute' or 'immanent' Trinity. His conclusions are characteristically inclusive, seeking to combine both a concern for the inner relationships of God as Trinity, as Father, Son and Holy Spirit, and for the outcome of these relationships in terms of human being and the life of the world. He takes a similar line to Rahner in affirming that, 'We know about the

Father, Son and Spirit as divine "Persons" only through the figure and disposition of Jesus Christ. Thus we can agree with the principle, often enunciated today, that it is only on the basis of the economic Trinity that we can have knowledge of the immanent Trinity and dare to make statements about it'. However, although the economic Trinity serves to interpret the immanent Trinity, it cannot simply be 'identified' with it, 'for the latter grounds and support the former. Otherwise the immanent, eternal Trinity would threaten to dissolve into the economic' and 'God would be swallowed up in the world process . . . ' (*TD3*: 508).

What von Balthasar is proposing is something entirely different, a theo-drama enacted on the world stage which finds its ultimate meaning as it is drawn into the eternal relationships of the divine Trinity in heaven. To this end he returns to the two dramatic triads which he outlined in the first volume. In the first triad of 'Dramatic Creativity', in the relationship between author, actor and director, von Balthasar suggests that we find 'a perfect metaphor for the economic Trinity in the theo-drama' (*TD3*: 532). But this cannot be separated from the second triad of 'Dramatic Realisation', of presentation, audience and horizon, enabling us to see how God is not simply *above* the drama but is also present *within* it. 'No longer does the Father sit unmoved, as Judge, on his throne high above the play; now his "script" is his own bending-down to the suffering creature in the form of Son and Spirit.' 'Thus the two triads of the *Prolegomena* merge into each other. The first triad, lit up with inner radiance, reveals the immanent-economic Trinity; the second is simply the way in which this Trinity, guiding and fashioning the world drama, draws it into itself' (*TD3*: 535).

4.4 *THE ACTION*

The two volumes dealing with the *dramatis personae* have shown us von Balthasar's theodramatic approach to anthropology and christology. Now, in Volume IV, von Balthasar offers his account of *The Action* and it is here that we find his soteriology. It begins 'Under the Sign of the Apocalypse' with a quite breathtaking account of the Book of Revelation. For von Balthasar, Revelation offers the most clearly theodramatic perspective to be found anywhere in the biblical witness. It offers 'a window into the ever-greater world of God' (*TD4*: 18), a unique vision which encompasses heaven and earth, time and eternity, mercy and wrath, the Old and New Covenants, all of which is centred upon the worship of the Lamb who was slain. 'What is dramatic in revelation is to be found in its specific uniqueness; namely that God is at the same time superior to history and involved in it.' This is reflected in the tension between Christ's atoning death on the Cross and its fulfilment in the coming of a new heaven and earth which is yet to be fully revealed. It also leads to what von Balthasar terms the 'specifically theological law of proportionate polarization', a description of that theological reality whereby 'the more God intervenes, the more he elicits opposition to him' (*TD4*: 51). Thus the dominant theme of this confrontation is 'fire', a fire which is 'dramatic in a heightened sense: God no longer deals with man from without but – by becoming man – from within man and at man's innermost level; Jesus is the man who burns with God's fire' (*TD4*: 60).

In his account of *The Action* von Balthasar seeks to do three things. In the first place, he picks up some of the themes arising from his theodramatic anthropology in Volume II, to show where the action can and must take place in terms of 'the *Pathos* of the World Stage' arising from the drama of human existence. Then he goes on to show how it is that Christ, 'acting from within God's Pathos', intervenes to overcome the inability of human efforts to resolve these issues and recover its true freedom and purpose. Finally, he endeavours to demonstrate how this saving drama can be accepted and appropriated by faithful Christians in the life of the Church and in the world. Or as von Balthasar himself puts it:

> In the first, Adam, man, unfolds his action, both as an individual and as community. In the second, God acts; first he prepares the way for Jesus Christ, then he acts in him, and then – most of all – he acts in him on the Cross and in his Resurrection. In the third, God and man encounter one another in history, in what the Book of Revelation has described as the Battle of the Logos. (*TD4*: 67)

For von Balthasar, the crucial paradox at the heart of human existence is our inability as finite and limited creatures to comprehend the issue of infinite and absolute being. The result is that 'man's historical situation in this world is in a state of permanent tension: he is constantly on the lookout for a solution, a redemption, but can never anticipate or construct it from his own resources; nor does he even have an intimation of it' (*TD4*: 75). Von Balthasar goes on to identify 'the wounds that existence bears' and how these 'aspects, that is, death, freedom, power and evil, sharpen the problem of existence to the point of rendering it unbearable' following which 'all human life becomes an uninterrupted, chaotic searching and feeling after a totality of meaning' (*TD4*: 77).

For von Balthasar, this searching after meaning has to involve three areas which he deals with in turn, namely 'The Claim of Finitude', 'Time and Death' and 'Freedom, Power and Evil'. Von Balthasar has little positive to offer as regards the first conundrum (in which he also addresses the 'mirage of progress'); 'it is impossible to unravel the paradox whereby man is forever trying to translate what is absolute into terms that are relative and transitory' (*TD4*: 94). Nor is he any more optimistic about the next problem. 'Everything we shall say here concerning man's time and man's death will only reinforce the paradox of existence, namely the endeavour to express the absolute through the relative' (*TD4*: 95). The bodily nature of human existence means that 'I am always thrown back into a fundamental solitude in which my death . . . is unavoidably getting nearer and nearer' (*TD4*: 96). Von Balthasar maintains that all human drama is concerned with appropriating 'the point of balance' between the conflicting claims of the absolute and the transitory, in the course of which human beings learn various 'gestures' such as 'conversion', 'forgiveness', 'love' and 'hope'; but since this is a balance which can only be established by God, the attempt is ultimately futile. 'Death is the ultimate limit of experience; existence gesticulates in the face of death, and death is its innermost certainty' (*TD4*: 117).

A similar paradox is thrown up in the complex relationship which exists between freedom, power and evil. Von Balthasar maintains that humanity is aware that 'evil in the world comes from freedom, a freedom that uses whatever power is available' and also that 'power is not intrinsically evil but contains a temptation to evil in so far as it represents a means of domination' (*TD4*: 137). The problem then arises with misuse of that finite freedom which has been granted to human being; it is intended for them to discover the fulfilment of their created and limited freedom in obedience to the unlimited and absolute freedom of God. But in so far as it also allows them to assert their independence and freedom of choice, it also allows for that pursuit of individual autonomy which results in the pursuit of power and emergence of evil. It is this development which von Balthasar characterizes as 'man's revolt against his essential structure', as 'the self tries to prescind from its rootedness in God and establish its own autonomy' and in so doing, rather than consolidating its freedom, is instead 'attempting to seize power' (*TD4*: 147). This is the 'primal temptation, autonomy' in which 'the one who chooses sets himself up as the standard of the good, thus subordinating goodness to his own exercise of power' (*TD4*: 151) – as opposed to the one who 'knows his personal autonomy is a gift and allows the image of God to radiate through him' (*TD4*: 155).

In turn this leads von Balthasar into an exploration of 'sin', in the course of which he shares Barth's underlining of its seriousness and unbearable reality, in that 'it is God *himself* who, in the life of Jesus Christ, undertakes to carry out the wrathful judgement upon sin' (*TD4*: 161). He also reflects on the growing 'intensification' of sin throughout the Bible, in line with his 'law of proportionate polarization' (mentioned earlier), noting that '*in the whole of history, Israel is the place where the nature and the burden of sin is most directly manifested*' (*TD4*: 173), and how in the New Testament 'sin is portrayed as a final intensification of the Old Testament No to God's Word (now made flesh)' (*TD4*: 177). Following on from this von Balthasar goes on to address the subject of 'Original Sin' and then 'Guilt and the World's Suffering' before offering his summary of the 'pathos' that takes place on the 'world stage'.

'We have endeavoured to show what the dramatic action (the play) looks like from the perspective of finite, time-bound man, in his subjection to death, free to commit evil and implicated in the world's suffering.' From such a predicament von Balthasar is clear that humankind is unable to extricate itself. 'His attempt to manufacture a redeemed existence out of all this – and this is the attempt of all nonbiblical religions that try to break out of the structures that govern earthly existence – is bound to lead, if it is consistently followed through, to man's self-dissolution'

(*TD4*: 201). Who then can save humanity from itself, and in such a way that the realities of finitude, time and death, the conditions of creatureliness, are not simply negated but given a new value and meaning?

The answer to all this is given when the chief Actor appears on stage (and the fact that he is introduced by reference to Anselm's *Cur Deus homo?* is not without significance). From what he has outlined so far, it is clear that it is only someone willing to take on himself those same constraints of finitude, time and death who can help save humankind from what St Paul calls 'the law of sin and death'. But at the same time it is only a divine initiative which can free humankind from the unresolved predicament of human existence, in the person of God-man, Jesus Christ. Von Balthasar's approach to the atonement thus draws on all that he has previously set out in terms of anthropology (man in God) and christology (persons in Christ).

Von Balthasar begins the second part of this volume with a brief account of 'The Long Patience of God', in which he reflects, as did the Fathers, on why Christ should have entered history at the time he did, and what interpretation should be made of the theodramatic character of the time which went before. His answer is that the 'best way is to hold fast to Israel's religious history, which in one respect has been lifted out from the "nations" and presented as a model', a model which both '*demonstrates* the relationship between divine and human freedom and *exercises* this relationship through the course of history' (*TD4*: 210). What Israel does then is to model 'the "twilight" nature of all pre-Christian religions' (*TD4*: 216) and thus, as the tension increases within its own framework of election and covenant, it points to 'the mystery of atonement', to 'the event of Jesus Christ as the solution to the pre-Christian impasse' (*TD4*: 229).

Von Balthasar's account of the atonement itself is governed by five themes which he finds to be central to the New Testament witness: namely that (1) God's 'only Son' has '*given himself up* for us all', (2) 'to the extent of *exchanging places with us*', thus (3) (negatively) *freeing* us from sin and death , (4) (positively) *drawing* us into '*the divine trinitarian life*' and (5) in all of which 'the entire reconciliation process is attributed to God's merciful *love*' (*TD4*: 240–4). Having established these biblical themes, he proceeds to examine how they have been treated in subsequent theology, for it is his judgment that the whole history of soteri-ology (and indeed the relative success of the various accounts to explain it) depends on the ability to keep all these different themes in play and in relationship with each other. Any 'one-sided' approach will 'infallibly result in a loss of theo-dramatic tension in the whole' (*TD4*: 244).

In the patristic period, von Balthasar observes that it is the second of these themes, that of the *exchange* which dominates, largely because of the need, following the christological heresies, to affirm both the full divinity and humanity of Christ (*TD4*: 244–54). However, turning to the mediaeval period, particularly under the influence of Anselm, it is the third of the motifs, that of *ransom* or *satisfaction*, which emerges as most influential (*TD4*: 255–66). Coming to the modern period, von Balthasar identifies the two dominant themes as being those of *solidarity* and *substitution*. Solidarity takes its cue from Jesus' humanity and public ministry; substitution from Jesus' divinity, his aton-ing death and resurrection. As part of his survey, von Balthasar includes a lengthy excursus on Rahner's soteriology, exploring the strengths and weaknesses of his approach in terms of the theme of 'solidarity' and coming to the conclusion that, 'Like all systems that fail to take the *sacrum commercium* seriously, Rahner's soteriology lacks the decisive dramatic element' (*TD4*: 283). He also examines Martin Luther's radicalizing of the substitutionary motif to see how in subsequent Protestant theo-logians this has led to the development of a theory of 'vicarious punishment' or penal suffering, which can be found in the writings of Barth, Pannenberg and Moltmann. Finally, he picks up Rene Girard's exploration of the 'Scapegoat' mechanism, based on the notion that 'All religious ritual is rooted in the scapegoat' (*TD4*: 299), (in the process of which von Balthasar notes how such approaches to 'religion' and a 'natural knowl-edge of God' are just what led Barth to condemn the 'analogy of being' as '*the* invention of the Antichrist'! (*TD4*: 308)).

What von Balthasar is concerned to show is that only a theodramatic theory of the atonement will suffice to allow all five themes to play their proper role.

For no element may be excluded here: God's entire world-drama is concentrated on and hinges on this scene. This is the theo-drama into which the world *and* God have their ultimate input; here absolute freedom enters into created freedom, interacts with created freedom, and acts *as* created freedom. (*TD4*: 318)

It also means that a 'Dramatic Soteriology' also needs to find space for these biblical themes as well as the 'valid and fruitful motifs' that have arisen in the history of theology and this he does in four steps.

In 'The Cross and the Trinity', von Balthasar affirms the need for three things: a doctrine of the Trinity which, in the relationship of mutual self-giving and trust between Father and Son through the Spirit, allows for the integration of solidarity and substitution in the life and death of Christ for us; an understanding of covenant, as the affirmation of the created order as part of the redeeming purpose of the divine Creator; and finally an appreciation of sacrament, as the model of self-offering and sacrifice, so characteristic of the life of the divine Trinity, is taken up and appropriated in the life of the Church and for the world. In the course of this he also discusses the relationship between the immanent and economic Trinity in light of Rahner's celebrated statement that 'The economic Trinity *is* the immanent Trinity and vice versa'. Von Balthasar's response is that from a theodramatic perspective the key is a 'kenotic' understanding of the Trinity:

it is the drama of the 'emptying' of the Father's heart, in the generation of the Son, that contains and surpasses all possible drama between God and a world. For any world only has its place within that distinction between Father and Son that is maintained and bridged by the Holy Spirit. (*TD4*: 327)

In 'Sin and the Crucified' von Balthasar addresses the issue of 'representation' and what it means to say that Christ died '*pro nobis*', for us, picking up on the biblical theme of the 'wondrous exchange': how in the Cross 'the God-man drama reaches its acme' as 'perverse finite freedom casts all its guilt onto God, making him the sole accused, the scapegoat, while God allows himself to be thoroughly affected by this, not only in the humanity of Christ, but also in Christ's trinitarian mission' (*TD4*: 335);

how this account must also include (with Barth) an understanding of 'God's wrath', for all that this must also be seen in context of 'the eternal, trinitarian love relationship between Father and Son' (*TD4*: 348); and how this is 'mediated' to the Church through the person of Mary, whose consent to Jesus' birth and death represents at one and the same time 'the fruit of Israel's positive history', Jesus' 'solidarity with all sinners' and the whole human race, and 'the response of the Church' *TD4*: 352–61). Mary's reception of Jesus' words from the Cross, 'Woman, behold your son' and 'Son, behold your mother' are a pointer to the way Christians receive his resurrection life, as the community gathered around Mary becomes the Church, Christ's gift of himself to the world; and so 'thus the Word finally and definitively becomes flesh in the Virgin-Mother, Mary-Ecclesia' (*TD4*: 361).

This process is drawn out more fully in the final two steps. In 'Resurrection, Spirit and Life in God' (*TD4*: 361–88), von Balthasar sets out the way the Risen Christ gives others a share in his drama by communicating his Spirit to them, liberating them from the 'principalities and powers' but also thereby freeing them to participate in the trinitarian life through baptism and the call to discipleship. Then in 'The Church and the Paschal Mystery' he explores the sacramental dimension to all of this, both in the Eucharist and in the '*communio sanctorum*', the communion of saints. The freedom which has been granted to humanity

> is perfected by the grace of a sublime participation in the absolute, divine freedom. This comes about through our being incorporated into the Eucharist that, in the Spirit, Christ makes to the Father. And it is precisely in participating in Christ's mission that our elevated freedom is placed at the service of the communion of saints. (*TD4*: 406)

And then, since 'the Church, as Bride and Body of Christ, shares in the "merits" of her Head's entire life and suffering, she is one with him in becoming the world's "sacrament of salvation"' (*TD4*: 422).

We now turn to the final part of 'The Action' in the 'The Battle of the Logos', in which von Balthasar explores its impact on the world in which we live. His starting point is that although Jesus 'stands in world history as God's representative' and 'emerges from this battle victorious, through his death on the Cross, his *descensus* and his Resurrection . . . this does not mean that all his work is done' (*TD4*: 427). The decisive battle has been fought but the war is still to be won. Jesus' warnings about the tribulations to come remains just as valid as they were when first uttered and any attempt to divide the history of the Church and the world since Christ into 'periods', or to identify a map of 'progress', remains a fruitless undertaking.

That is because the 'Provocation offered by Jesus', which von Balthasar describes in terms of a 'Gathering and Separating' and then 'Gathering and Sifting', remains active and in play. This can be no surprise in light of the Jesus who came proclaiming, 'He who is not with me is against me, and who does not gather with me scatters (Mt. 12.30; Lk 11.23, quoted in *TD4*: 433). Jesus did not come 'imagining that he could gather without introducing division'. Von Balthasar reminds us not be afraid of the 'harsh truth' that in 'making his provocative claim to have reconciled the world in God, Jesus never suggested he was creating an earthly paradise'. What we see in the present time is that 'intensifying of the dramatic confrontation' which is 'only possible in the post-Christian age, when the diffuse religious dimension . . . has become subordinated to the No to the claim of Jesus, who concentrates everything "religious" on himself: "No one comes to the Father except by me"' (*TD4*: 442–3).

Nor can the Church which bears Christ's name and shares his life be spared the same conflict. Her share in the struggle is described in the 'The Church's Form: Beautiful and Marred'. 'The Church is a community of sinners who have been sanctified through baptism; the sinfulness that continues to adhere to them or reawakens within them leads naturally to conflict' (*TD4*: 453). Thus the Christian Church has to encounter both the emergence of other religions which deny Christ's sovereignty and also the rise of philosophical traditions which assert instead the autonomy of human rationality. More damaging than this, she has also to address the reality of heresy and schism in her own ranks, for whatever the progress made in terms of ecumenical relationships and goodwill, the fact of Christian disunity remains a scandal.

In concrete terms, Christ only exists together with the community of saints united in the *Immaculata*, together with the communion of the ministerial office visibly united in Peter and his successors and together with the living, ongoing tradition united in the great councils and declarations of the Church. Where these elements of integration are rejected in principle, it is impossible to return to unity, however much good will is played by the partners. (*TD4*: 456)

This struggle is 'no mere battle of words and ideas between human beings'; rather it is here that 'mankind is drawn into the theodramatic war that has broken out between God, in his Logos, and hell's anti-logos' (*TD4*: 463). In this struggle, von Balthasar asserts that the only path which leads to real freedom is that of the 'Slain and Victorious' Christ. By way of contrast he picks up on two ways in which the Catholic Church has tried to proclaim a message of freedom in more worldly terms under the heading 'Theodramatic Dimensions of Liberation'. He refers both to a Vatican 2 constitution '*Gaudium et Spes*' and to the developments of 'liberation theology' – but ultimately remains critical of both; the encyclical assumes an 'ideal convergence' between the 'one-world culture' and the 'catholicity of the Church's mission' which von Balthasar considers 'highly abstract' (and by implication dubious) while 'liberation theology' assumes means and ends which appear to run counter to the Cross. Von Balthasar asks the question; 'Can the Cross of Christ be changed into a "tactical instrument" in issues that are purely this-worldly?' (*TD4*: 484).

Von Balthasar's response to all this is to reassert the need to return to the 'central fact' which can not be circumvented or ignored. It is the fact that 'Jesus by his obedient death takes over the guilty death that is our fate' (*TD4*: 495). It is this death which von Balthasar maintains can alone address the challenge posed by death to human meaning and existence (in the process revisiting 'the seven facets of death in the human drama' outlined in his *Prolegomena* to show how 'all of them are marvellously enfolded in the unique, peerless death of Jesus' (*TD4*: 497)). Moreover, it is in bearing witness to this atoning death that human beings can play their part in the 'Battle of the Logos'. 'So the martyrs can go to their death rejoicing because of the representation performed on the Cross, but they owe this courage to the anguish of him who wrestled on the Mount of Olives . . .' (*TD4*: 502).

4.5 *THE LAST ACT*

This struggle reaches its culmination in the final volume of von Balthasar's *Theo-Drama*, in which he offers his eschatology. However, since this work is subtitled a 'theo-dramatic theory', it is not so much about *ta eschata,* the last things, but rather *The Last Act*. As with his account of 'the Action' in the previous volume, it is heavily influenced by his reading of Johannine theology, which von Balthasar regards as the most thoroughly theo-dramatic in the New Testament and which, in the Book of Revelation, is most clearly borrowing from and reinterpreting themes and motifs from the Old Testament. But it is also, perhaps more so than any of the other volumes, heavily influenced by the mystical visions of his companion Adrienne von Speyr, as is evident from the extensive quotations and references to her work which are found throughout the volume.

By way of an 'introduction' Von Balthasar begins his last volume with the 'the Idea of a Christian Eschatology' (*TD5*: 19–54), during which he reflects on three of the themes which have influenced it, addressing in turn 'late-Jewish "apocalyptic" expectation of an imminent end of the world', 'Jesus' own expectation' and 'the primitive Church's expectation of the imminent end of the world and the return of Christ' (*TD5*: 19). His conclusion, after consideration of these various approaches, is that '*the New Testament no longer entertains the idea of a self-unfolding horizontal theo-drama; there is only a vertical theo-drama in which every moment of time, insofar as it has christological significance, is directly related to the Exalted Lord, who has taken the entire content of all history – life, death and resurrection – with him into the supra-temporal realm*' (*TD5*: 48). Within this, it is von Balthasar's reading of Johannine Christology, with its emphasis upon that realised eschatology inaugurated by the presence of Christ, which underpins his own theological enterprise. 'For John, the Christ-event, which is always seen in its totality, is the vertical irruption of the fulfilment into horizontal time; such irruption does not leave this time – with its present, past and future – unchanged, but draws it into itself and thereby gives it a new character' (*TD5*: 25).

For at the heart of this last volume lies the question: 'How is it that "the World" which is "from God" can become "the World in God"?' In his opening section 'The World is from God', von Balthasar makes it clear that it is 'the Trinity and not Christology' which is 'the last horizon of the revelation of God in himself and in his dramatic relationship with the world'. This in turn means that 'we may only discuss the anthropological *eschata* – traditionally man's death, judgment and final destiny – within the framework of a theocentric eschatology' (*TD5*: 56). This will involve two things: first 'a new understanding of the dramatic interplay between God and man' on the basis of the *imago trinitatis* in the creature', in that the final destiny of human being is to share in the triune life of God; and secondly a new understanding of the relationship between God's time and human time, in particular the 'primacy' of 'God's "time"' over creaturely or human time in light of 'Christ's "time"'. And ultimately this will all mean that 'the real "last thing" is the triune life of God disclosed in Jesus Christ' (*TD5*: 57).

It is this theme that von Balthasar addresses in the 'The World is from the Trinity' (*TD5*: 61–109). He starts from the scholastic understanding that 'creation is embraced within the Trinity, which is its inalienable precondition' (*TD5*: 61) and then from the perspective of the New Testament in which 'the revelation of God that takes place in Jesus Christ is primarily a trinitarian one: Jesus does not speak about God in general but shows us the Father and gives us the Holy Spirit'. In turn this means that, 'All earthly becoming is a reflection of the eternal "happening" in God, which, we repeat, is *per se* identical with the eternal Being or essence' (*TD5*: 67). Von Balthasar's conclusion from this is that 'all creaturely being and becoming is oriented to the eternal, incarnate Son: everything is on its way to him' and this brings us back to 'the fact that the Son's eternal *processio*, which carries out God's plan for the world, is identical with the Son's *missio*' (*TD5*: 80).

This trinitarian revelation also shows how 'the fact that "the Other" exists is *absolutely good*', and how this is 'a truth that, by analogy, also applies to creation' (*TD5*: 81). For it is this divine 'letting go' which creates the time and space for creation to come into being in the first place; 'its primal origin in the Trinity lies in the way in which the Persons of the Trinity "make room" (space) for one another, granting each other freedom of being and action' (*TD5*: 93). It follows from this that 'the idea of the world is from God and in God' and furthermore that 'everything that is in process of becoming, within the world's total becoming, has a somehow indefinite profile until it attains its definitive shape, ultimately in full participation in the life of the Trinity' (*TD5*: 100–01).

It is this process of becoming which von Balthasar addresses next, under the heading, 'Earth moves Heavenward'. He reminds us that both earth and heaven are part of creation and stand in relationship to God, though within this relationship there is a 'priority' to heaven. 'Not only has heaven given earth the ability to transcend itself and move towards heaven, it is always supporting it in its journey toward fulfilment' (*TD5*: 116). Moreover, 'the union between earth and heaven in Christ presupposes God's triune nature. This is because the Son on earth cannot represent his own divine nature . . . rather he translates his eternal relationship with the Father into the terms of time and creatureliness' (*TD5*: 120). In this work, the Church has her own distinctive role to play; she is 'the prolongation of Christ's mediatorial nature and work . . . she lives objectively (in her institution and her sacraments) and subjectively (in her saints and, fundamentally, in all her members) in the interchange between heaven and earth' (*TD5*: 131). 'So it is that all subjective efforts within the Church share in the same life, which is a transition from earth to heaven' (*TD5*: 137).

There follows a discussion of the 'Shape of Christian Hope'. For von Balthasar, 'it follows that Christian hope is *vertical*, since it is grounded in the Christ-event which is now "above"' (*TD5*: 147). But there remains the issue as to how far it can be represented horizontally, in terms of human history and here von Balthasar examines the writings of the French Jesuit, Teilhard de Chardin and the German Protestant theologian, Jürgen Moltmann (*TD5*: 152–180). Both writers seek to offer a theological basis for a Christian hope that can speak to the contemporary world. But in both attempts he finds their work compromised by the presence of assumptions which come from other sources: in the attempt to correlate theology with developments in evolutionary biology in Teilhard de Chardin; and with the materialism of Ernst Bloch in Moltmann's *Theology of Hope*. In de Chardin, the 'one-sidedly incarnational emphasis puts the theology of the Cross – the work of atonement wrought by the Trinity – almost entirely in the shade', while in Moltmann, the emphasis on the Cross and 'the negativity of estrangement from God that Christ there endures' serves to obscure 'the positive archetypes found, within the Trinity, of the *imagines trinitatis* in the world and in salvation history' (*TD5*: 167 & 173). Von Balthasar's conclusion is that, 'Christian hope, theological hope, goes beyond this world, but it does not pass it by: rather it takes the world with it on its way to God, who has graciously prepared a dwelling in himself for us and for the world' (*TD5*: 176).

In the second part of this volume, von Balthasar looks at three 'Aspects of the Final Act' in terms of how it engages with 'Tragedy', how it is set within the 'trinitarian Drama', and then how within this 'Man' is upheld by 'God's Undergirding'. He begins by addressing 'The Final Act as Tragedy' recognizing that there is a danger that his account thus far could appear 'somewhat triumphalist'. His specific concern is to register the possibility that God's freely grace may be rejected and 'a part of this creation, supposedly designed for heaven' will instead be consigned 'to eternal perdition' (*TD5*: 191). This leads him to examine the concept of Judgement as it is found in the Old Testament, in the Synoptics and Paul, and then in the Johannine tradition, in which he finds the 'turning point' of the drama. 'The abyss of divine love that we see in the Father's sending of the Son to save the world (3: 16) brings what is implacably hostile to God, what is devilish, out into the open' (*TD5*: 203). He concludes with an exploration of what is meant by the Devil and ends by agreeing with Barth's conclusion that, 'there is not, and cannot be, a transparent doctrine of the demonic'. 'The mysteries of God are much more exposed to us than the mysteries of evil.' (*TD5*: 207). However, the enduring reality of evil does still provide a problem; it reminds us of an 'eschatological "tragedy" in the very midst of "God's victory"' insofar as 'a portion of God's plan for the world has failed, a portion of his creation has turned out to be meaningless' (*TD5*: 212).

This leads von Balthasar to address a topic of growing theological interest, and one that emerges in contrast to the traditional doctrine of divine impassibility, namely the 'Pain of God'. He starts by suggesting that the position of the Fathers is much more 'nuanced' than is always understood before going on to survey some more recent interpretations, including Hegel, Moltmann, Koch and Kitamori. Interestingly, he again includes

Barth, whose account of 'God's Trinitarian Suffering in Christ' offers a distinctive way forward because of 'the deliberately christological foundation' he lays in terms of Christ and Election (*TD5*: 236). However, 'Barth's reticence in the field of the divine processions within the Trinity will not allow him to go any farther here' (*TD5*: 239). Notwithstanding Barth's dismissal of the possibility 'whether God in his *theologia* can really be influenced by his *oikonomia*' (*TD5*: 244) (i.e. whether the internal relations of the Trinity can be read from God's external relations to the world) von Balthasar considers that this is an issue which must be addressed, albeit with great caution.

Accordingly it is this topic he addresses in his next chapter, subtitled 'A Trinitarian Drama'. The thrust of his argument is that we can only make sense of the 'Pain of God' if we approach it as a drama which takes place primarily between the Persons of the Trinity and in which, through the mission of the Son, human creatures are invited to participate. Thus, 'this "economic" reality is only the expression of something "immanent" in the Trinity' (*TD5*: 258) so that the apparent tensions in the mission of Christ between death and life, sorrow and joy, union and separation, can be seen in terms of that deeper relationship which holds the Persons of the Trinity together in mutual love and freedom. This is true even in the apparent dereliction of the Cross and when Christ passes through hell on Holy Saturday (and here von Balthasar draws heavily on the mystical insights of Adrienne von Speyr). 'The mystery of Good Friday and Holy Saturday is thus a mystery of the loneliness of love between Father and Son in the Spirit . . . ' (*TD5*: 269).

A second and related issue is that of 'The Question of Universal Salvation', which would appear 'to empty God's involvement in the world of every last trace of tragedy' (*TD5*: 269). Once again Barth is a principal dialogue partner for von Balthasar, as 'Barth's great "doctrine of election" . . . represents the breakthrough that brought the discussion into being' (*TD5*: 270). Von Balthasar is very sympathetic to Barth's approach and wants to affirm both the 'comprehensive' nature of that redemption witnessed in the Pauline and Johannine writings and also its christological foundation. He maintains that there is 'nothing partial in Christ's suffering and dying' and that 'since everyone is created with a view to Christ, God applies to them the measuring rod of Christ's unconditional life', again quoting Adrienne von Speyr (*TD5*: 284). However, this still means that 'we come up against the *Mysterium iniquitatis*' (the mystery of evil), for this is 'the central mystery of the theo-drama: God's heightened love provokes a heightened hatred that is as bottomless as love itself (Jn 15.25)' (*TD5*: 285). For von Balthasar, 'hell would be what is finally condemned by God; what is left is sin, which has been separated from the sinner by the work of the Cross' (*TD5*: 314). What then is the right approach to this question? 'If we look back from this vantage point to the judgment that awaits every sinful human being, the appropriate attitude will be a hope that is not without a certain fear'(*TD5*: 321).

In the final chapter in this section he engages with 'Man in God's Understanding' and looks again at the issues of death and judgement in the light of Christ's death and resurrection. For von Balthasar, the possibility of 'genuine liberation from the tragedy of death' 'lies in the fact that the human destiny of death is undergirded by the death of Christ' (*TD5*: 325). In biblical terms this 'undergirding death' is interpreted in two ways: 'On the one hand, this death takes the place of all sinful deaths . . . However, this *deed* on God's part contains the second aspect, namely the *teaching* that this deed is the proclamation of an absolute love . . . that originates in the triune being of God' (*TD5*: 327). Jesus' representative death means for the Christian both 'living in Christ's death, Christ's life' and 'dying into Christ's life, Christ's death'. It also implies that 'acknowledging that our death has a relationship with Christ's death is simply identical with the act of faith in which we point our entire being – living or dying – away from ourselves and relate it to the life and death of Christ' (*TD5*: 342).

Von Balthasar goes further to address this subject of judgement by affirming that 'there can only be one single Judgement, including and embracing all individual judgments' (*TD5*: 360). He also affirms that this can include a proper place for the traditional Catholic teaching on purification, since 'purgatory comes into existence on Holy Saturday, when the Son walks through "hell", introducing the element of mercy into the condition of those who are justly lost' and thus has its origins in the Cross (*TD5*: 363). However, and true to his overall theme, his final word is that 'the *eschaton* is not man but the triune God, who in

Christ's Cross, descent into hell, and Resurrection, undergirds all human activity – whether it be sin or love' (*TD5*: 368).

We then return to the third and final theme of this volume which is 'The World in God', and here von Balthasar begins by examining it under the heading, 'Embedded in God'. His starting point is to view the world in terms of the death and resurrection of Jesus, in 'He ascends to prepare a place for us'; for 'in the movement from earth to heaven, it is his death (in which his Resurrection is hiddenly present) that holds earth and heaven together *and* holds them apart' (*TD5*: 376). But within this there is equally a sacramental dimension, in that Christ's 'crucified and risen body' is also a 'eucharistically shared body' (*TD5*: 381) from which it follows that 'beholding and inwardly participating in the Son in his eucharistic self-giving, becomes a beholding and participating in the life of the Trinity' (*TD5*: 384).

However, such participation does not involve a loss of creaturely being. 'There can be no question . . . of the world moving from a position "outside God" to a position "inside God": instead there must be a change in the condition of the world while it remains close to, and immanent in, God' (*TD5*: 395). The 'embedding' to which von Balthasar refers, means for the creature that 'the way they are contained in God provides us with a measure for their creaturely form', one given them 'purely by grace as an ontological space in which to exist' (*TD5*: 399). And so within this participation there is also preserved that creaturely freedom which is 'fundamental to our argument' (and to the working out of the theo-drama) 'namely that creaturely freedom is a mystery inseparable from the dignity of the person; it must be preserved in eternal life' (*TD5*: 403–04). Von Balthasar then goes on to explore the relationship between heaven and earth in terms of 'Reciprocity', picking up on the two themes of eucharist and harvest and the way in which they both point to the reality that 'in heaven we shall live the full and eternal content of what on earth was present only as a transcendent unsatisfiable longing' (*TD5*: 413).

The final chapter in this section deals with the question of what it means to participate 'in the Triune Life'. Characteristically, von Balthasar begins by affirming that this is an 'absolute mystery' before going on to examine three ways in which this 'participation, which is at the core of eternal blessedness' (*TD5*: 428) has been addressed in the history of theology: first in St John of the Cross who explores how 'the breathing of the Holy Spirit by Father and Son also becomes a breathing on the part of the soul' (*TD5*: 432); prior to St John is the teaching of 'divine birth' in the Son offered by Eckhart and the Rhineland mystics; but before them all is the teaching of the Fathers about the birth of the Logos in Mary, and through Mary in the Church, 'a process that begins with baptism (thus the Fathers) and unfolds in the Christian's progress in perfection here and now (thus the mystics)' (*TD5*: 469).

In all of this, von Balthasar believes, 'we have been exploring the depths of what theology, all too abruptly, calls "*visio beatifica*"' (the beatific vision). This is 'a participation in the life of God himself' but as such also 'a completion and perfection of something that began in the Incarnation of the Logos' (*TD5*: 470). He finishes this chapter with an exploration of this participation in terms of the twin eucharistic themes of 'Meal and Marriage'. In particular he explores the way 'this divine gift is offered to the world as meal and as marriage, mediating the life of the Trinity, but also as a concrete, prototypical realization of early existence . . . It is mortal men who receive the eucharistic food as *pharmakon athanasias* (the medicine of immortality), and it is a visible, earthly Church, that Christ the Bridegroom purifies though Cross and baptism and presents to himself as his Bride' (*TD5*: 478). However, this bridal and spousal relationship is not 'some Idealist process' hovering over the world, but rather one which 'takes place in world time'. For, 'the world, both inside and outside the Church is always resisting being transformed into the Body of Christ' and 'this means that crucifixion and the piercing of the heart are always going on, and God is ceaselessly wooing man in the Person of the Crucified who, for his part, can do nothing but take "all who receive him" with him unto his Cross' (*TD5*: 478–9).

Von Balthasar's closing reflections on his *Theo-Drama* come under the heading, 'If you comprehend it, it is not God' and so begin, appropriately with the mystery of God's dramatic purpose. For von Balthasar, it is quite clear that the 'only way to grasp the "figure" of Jesus, the central actor of the theo-drama, is by *not grasping* it and by allowing it to take its place in the "ungraspable" context of the mystery of the Trinity' (*TD5*: 492–3). This is because the salvation of the world can only be understood as a part of that greater trinitarian drama. 'If all these formulations are to have an abiding meaning, and if the paradoxes they contain are insurmountable, this meaning can only be found in the trinitarian character of truth itself' (*TD5*: 496). Indeed all this serves as a pointer to what von Balthasar will undertake in the third and final part of his trilogy, the *Theologic*, which we shall be examining in our next chapter.

However before this, von Balthasar has a final word to say about what he has attempted in this volume, namely the presentation of a 'trinitarian and christological eschatology' (*TD5*: 506). His way of approaching it has meant that many traditional questions have been turned on their head; for example, the question of eternal damnation, in anthropological terms 'What does man lose in losing God?' has here been put from God's perspective, in terms of 'What does God lose in losing man'. 'The whole thrust of this book has been to show that the infinite possibilities of divine freedom all lie *within* the trinitarian distinctions and are thus free possibilities within the eternal life of love in God *that has always been realized*' (*TD5*: 508).

Thus, the question about what has happened on earth has been explored in terms of what has and always is happening within the triune life of the God from whom all creation takes its being. 'From all eternity the divine "conversation" envisages the possibility of involving a non-divine world in the Trinity's love' and this conversation has always included the necessary, preliminary stages: 'the creation of finite freedom in its twofold relation (to God and to other free creatures)'; 'the Incarnation of the Son, which in turn draws the Church, and through her the world' into the mystery of the triune life; and then 'the Cross, which opens a path whereby men can get beyond their refusal and allow themselves to be drawn into God' (*TD5*: 509).

What then does God gain from the world? Von Balthasar's answer, in theodramatic terms, is 'a gift'. 'An additional gift, given to the Son by the Father, but equally a gift made by the Son to the Father, and by the Spirit to both. It is a gift because, through the distinct operations by each of the three Persons, the world acquires an inward share in the divine exchange of life; as a result the world is able to take the divine things it has received from God, together with the gift of being created, and return them to God as a divine gift' (*TD5*: 521).

CHAPTER 5

THEO-LOGIC

INTRODUCTION

Von Balthasar begins the third and final part of his trilogy with a 'General Introduction' in which he outlines his plan for the work. 'From first to last, the trilogy is keyed to the transcendental qualities of being, in particular to the analogy between their status and form in creaturely being, on the one hand, and in Divine Being, on the other.' This is reflected in the 'correspondence between worldly "beauty" and divine "glory" in the *Aesthetics* and between worldly, finite freedom and divine, infinite freedom in the *Drama*'. Following on from this, von Balthasar continues, 'our task in the present theological *Logos* will be to reflect upon the relationship between the structure of creaturely truth and the structure of divine truth'. For von Balthasar this is crucial. 'Without philosophy, there can be no theology' (*TL1*: 7).

Set out in this way, the task of the *Theo-Logic* would seem naturally to follow on from his *Theological Aesthetics* and *Theo-Drama*. In actual fact, the process was not quite so straightforward. The first volume of the *Theo-Logic* is essentially a re-publication of his 1947 book, *Truth of the World* and can perhaps best be read (see Dalzell, 1997: 37–8) as a response to the transcendental approach of his Jesuit colleague Karl Rahner. In particular, it offers a response to some of the issues raised by Rahner's book, *Spirit in the World*, for which von Balthasar wrote an extensive review when first published in 1939. He and Rahner had much in common, not least in terms of their Jesuit training and grounding in Thomist philosophy, and von Balthasar shared Rahner's concern both for the centrality of being in coming to a knowledge of God and for a properly integrated understanding of the relationship between grace and nature, as opposed to the much challenged 'extrinsicism' of scholastic theology.

However, there were other aspects of Rahner's theology about which von Balthasar was more critical. This criticism was to take public form much later in his attack on the notion of 'anonymous Christianity' in the aftermath of Vatican II, but his concerns go back earlier and centre on Rahner's re-interpretation of Aquinas, in the light of Kant and the Idealist tradition, in his *Spirit in the World*. In particular, he was critical of the way in which Rahner's focus on human subjectivity, following the work of Maréchal, appeared to downplay truth's dependence on the transcendent rationality of God. As Karen Kilby summarizes it; 'Both thinkers were trained in neo-scholasticism and both found it inadequate, but they moved away from it in different directions—very crudely put, Rahner moved away in the direction of the subject, and Balthasar in the direction of the object' (Oakes and Moss, 2004: 263).

Von Balthasar's concern was that such a narrow focus on the subject could obscure that wider vision of the totality of being upon which truth was grounded. His response was to offer an alternative epistemology of his own, focused on truth as one of the transcendentals of being. He set out the two stages of his task as follows. 'The first considers truth as we first encounter it in the world, as the truth of things and of man, a truth that ultimately points back to God the Creator . . . The second part considers the truth that God has made known to us about himself through revelation and which, once positively revealed, becomes the ultimate norm of all truth in the world' (*TL1*: 30). The first stage would use largely philosophical concepts and result in *Truth of the World*. The second stage would be delayed, for what von Balthasar called 'extrinsic, biographical reasons' (*TL1*: 10 and see our opening chapter) for some 40 years, until the publication of what will become the final two volumes of the *Theo-Logic*, in *Truth of God* and *The Spirit of Truth*.

These final two volumes will have a more clearly theological approach, offering a 'theological enquiry, which presupposes God's self-revelation in the divine, incarnate Logos and his expositor [*Ausleger*], the Pneuma, and focuses explicitly on this self-revelation as its object' (*TL1*: 13). They will also continue that critique of Rahner's transcendental approach which has been intimated earlier, as von Balthasar warns that, we will have to be aware of dividing it into a categorial revelation, on the one hand, and a transcendental revelation, on the other, as if we could interpret Christ, and the Spirit's exposition [*Auslegung*] of Christ in the Church, as a merely categorial sphere, which we could then distinguish from an overarching, pan-historical transcendental sphere. (*TL1*: 13)

For even in *Truth of the World* there is a strong theological thrust. Von Balthasar is clear not just that our understanding of truth comes out of a reflection on the nature of being, in which the limited and finite aspect of human knowledge and consciousness point towards the unlimited and infinite nature of being itself, but also that such reflection inevitably leads to the conclusion that truth is part of God's gracious self-communication to his creation, and that to participate in truth is to come to share in God's own being. His starting point is that 'man is not just a perceiver and an actor; he is also a thinker, speaker and formulator'. This means that 'our project has to conclude with a reflection on the possibility of expressing and justifying this *praxis* in human concepts and words'. In light of what has been demonstrated in the previous two parts of the trilogy, it also means that 'this enterprise . . . can succeed only on a trinitarian foundation' (*TL1*: 22). But in order to do this, von Balthasar has first to explore 'the structures of intra-worldly truth', which is the task he begins in *Truth of the World*.

5.1 *TRUTH OF THE WORLD*

In this earlier volume, von Balthasar explores the concept of truth under four headings, truth in turn as 'Nature', as 'Freedom', as 'Mystery' and as 'Participation'. In 'Truth as Nature' (*TL1*: 35–78), he starts from the basis that truth cannot be proved but is self-evident and must be assumed; 'Truth is as evident as existence and essence, as unity, goodness and beauty' (*TL1*: 35). He goes on to explore the notion of truth in terms which express what he calls its 'two-sidedness' or 'double nature'. Truth is the measure between being and appearance, its role expressed in the double relationship of 'unconcealment' (the Greek *aletheia*) and 'trustworthiness' (the Hebrew *emeth*). It depends upon the awareness and inter-relationship between subject and object, each of which in opening up to the other, becomes aware of its own self-consciousness, and at the same time of its own limited and finite existence in contrast to the unlimited and infinite nature of being itself. Thus in terms of human engagement and knowledge, it is 'the creature's analogical participation in the act by which God's archetypal, productive knowledge creatively metes out truth' (*TL1*: 78).

This emphasis upon relationship and reciprocity in truth is picked up in the next section, 'Truth as Freedom' (*TL1*: 79–130). In themselves, subject and object each have the freedom as to how much they choose to disclose or to hide, both in their self-communication to each other and in their willingness to accept the reliability of the truth they have received. This highlights the role of trustworthiness and the willingness of love to take responsibility for the fullness of truth, as opposed to that narrowing or partial truth which is less than the whole. 'Love is the selfless communication of what is mine and the selfless welcoming of the other in myself. It is thus the predetermined measure of all truth' (*TL1*: 123). In contrast to the 'abuse of truth' that makes 'the fragment sufficient to the detriment of the totality' and insists on 'partial standpoints and perspectives', love 'makes us see into the depths and into the heights. It orders and crystallizes finite truth around the pole of absolute truth' (*TL1*: 128–30).

In turn this leads on to the subject of the next section 'Truth as Mystery' (*TL1*: 131–225), in which the consequences of this emphasis upon truth as personal and relational are explored, using such headings as 'situation', 'perspective' and 'personality'. Reflecting on the interplay of 'word', 'significance' and 'image', von Balthasar suggests that the language used to communicate and refer to appearance points also towards that deeper mystery of being which lies behind it; how it is that Truth 'can be found only in a floating middle between the appearance and the thing that appears' (*TL1*: 138). Here we are moving into the same area which von Balthasar will explore in the first volume of his *Aesthetics*, as he discerns 'an especially close connection between this aspect of truth and the concept of beauty. For the name of this radiant property of truth, which overwhelms by its splendour, its indivisible integrity, and its perfect expressive power, is, in fact, none other than beauty'. This leads him to the conclusion that 'because of beauty truth is always intrinsically a matter of grace' (*TL1*: 141–2).

The final section, 'Truth as Participation' is the most explicitly theological of the four, in so far as it sets out the basis of the relationship between worldly and divine truth. Von Balthasar's conclusion is that 'if there is finite being and truth at all, it is only because of a free creative deed and utterance of God' and that 'this ontological dependence of finite truth can be inferred immediately from its "creatureliness", that is, from its contingency' (*TL1*: 229). Any affirmation of worldly truth has its ground in the free gift of God who chooses to communicate something of his truth in creation and thus enables his creatures to receive and to respond to that knowledge. Moreover, as human beings come to share in this disclosure of worldly truth, they discover pointers to the divine truth which lies behind and underpins all language and communication. All this is grounded in the supreme act of loving self-communication, which is God's revelation of himself in the Word made flesh. And it is this which makes speaking the truth an act of love. 'The truth is the measure of being, but love is the measure of truth' (*TL1*: 264).

Further examination of that truth will take up the second part of von Balthasar's task, even though as we have noted it will not be undertaken for another 40 years. However, even though this volume predates both his study of Barth and beginning of *The Glory of the Lord*, we can discern some of the influences which will help shape those works. This is evident, particularly in the way he draws on the key concepts which he has learnt from his mentor Przywara (namely polarity and the analogy of being), and also in the position which he takes on the relationship between nature and grace (and in turn faith and reason). Von Balthasar is clear from the start that 'the world as it concretely exists is one that is always already related either positively or negatively to the God of grace and supernatural revelation. There are no neutral points or surfaces in this relationship' (*TL1*: 30). This means in turn that there can be no standing outside of the grace of God or claiming that human rationality has access to the divine independently of God's revelation in Christ, the issue which is at the heart of Barth's allegations against natural theology and the analogy of being.

The influence of Przywara is revealed in his references to polarity. Polarity represents that tension between finite and infinite, personal and universal, spirit and matter, revealed and concealed which sums up much of human existence. Viewed in philosophical or existential terms such tensions offer a potentially explosive mix; however, when interpreted though the analogy of being, they point instead towards the absolute truth and being of God. 'This inner worldly polarity and analogy affecting the criterion of truth is rooted ultimately in a transcendent analogy between the divine and the worldly subject within the act of knowing itself' (*TL1*: 261). This points the way towards a proper interdependence of philosophy and theology and also to an appropriate participation in the truth of God. 'The analogy of truth, as participation and revelation, is thus fulfilled in the ever greater obedience of the creature to the decree of the ever greater God as he reveals himself ever anew in each situation.' It also points to the fact that; 'The truth of the world is grounded in the truth of God that reveals itself in it' (*TL1*: 244). It is this truth which von Balthasar will address in his next volume.

5.2 *TRUTH OF GOD*

'Theo-logic begins with the self-revelation of the triune God in the Incarnation of the divine Logos, and the Logos is the Word, the Son and the expositor [*Ausleger*] of the Father. It is as such that he understands himself and as such that he wishes to be understood. Yet who could understand him to be such if there were no *Pneuma* to lead us into the truth of the Logos and, therefore, into his relationship with the Father?' (*TL2*: 11). With these words, von Balthasar sets out his task for the final two volumes of the *Theo-Logic*. In Volume II, *Truth of God* he sets out the truth of the Incarnation in Jesus Christ, the 'Word made flesh', both in terms of *ana*-logic, that is the intimations of creaturely wisdom which point 'upwards' towards the divine, and *kata*-logic, the divine truth which is revealed in the Son's 'coming down' to earth. Then in Volume III, *The Spirit of Truth*, he will explore how the Holy Spirit interprets and expounds that truth. However, while it may appear that these volumes have in turn a christological and then a pneumatological focus, von Balthasar is clear that both tasks have to be done within a firmly trinitarian framework; 'we must never forget that the indivisible triune God performs all his saving deeds in unity, even as each hypostasis operates according to its proper being' (*TL2*: 11).

Characteristically, his way into this is through a 'Johannine entryway', for it is in John, and above all in the Prologue to John's Gospel, that the 'fullness' of this truth and its links to the 'glory' and 'goodness' of God are revealed. It is as the Word 'became flesh' and dwelt among us that 'we have beheld his glory, the glory as of the only Son from the Father, full of grace and truth' (Jn 1.14). For von Balthasar it follows that,

> Only when truth is conceived in christological-trinitarian terms can it be linked with the notion of 'fullness'. For it then includes, not only the other transcendentals on the ontological level ('glory', 'goodness', and, in the definitiveness of the enfleshed display of the divine Word, 'unity'), but also the Son's constitutive, indissoluble relationship to the Father and the Spirit on the trinitarian level. (*TL2*: 21)

In the next three chapters, von Balthasar explores this truth from an 'analogical' perspective, that is in terms of how human and creaturely logic points towards the truth to be revealed in the divine Word. Following on from the insights established in *Truth of the World*, he begins by affirming that this will be a 'logic of love'. Since the question about truth in theology has its object in God, and a God who in Jesus has become a God 'for and with us', this means that Jesus 'places thought, together with all the other faculties of the soul, in the service of divine love' (*TL2*: 27). He then goes on to show how various theologians and philosophers have posited a 'triadic structure' to 'worldly logic', from Augustine's reflections on the Trinity to Hegel's philosophy of being, to twentieth century dialogical theologians such as Buber and Ebner. Von Balthasar's own contribution is to express amazement that in this discussion 'the parent-child relationship is always lightly brushed aside' (*TL2*: 59) as the love of two people coming together to create a third 'remains, in spite of all the obvious dissimilarities, the most eloquent *imago Trinitatis* that we find woven into the fabric of the creature' (*TL2*: 62).

Von Balthasar then explores the 'Possibility of Christology', in terms of the question whether 'human logic' offers 'a strong enough basis to bear the weight of an authentic rendering of divine logic?' (*TL2*: 65). He does this first positively, in terms of the Logos who 'declares himself', and in terms of Christ's being an 'image' or 'icon' of God. However, this raises the paradox of a Jesus who is both 'wholly other and the same' (*TL2*: 68) and leads von Balthasar to explore in particular the parables of Jesus. Such stories require a level of recognition on a worldly basis, in order that they be heard and understood, and yet they also point to a deeper and divine truth which can only be perceived later. In this way the parables offer a prime example of how, as Jesus 'goes about expositing divine logic in human logic, the Logos does not find the latter unprepared' (*TL2*: 78). 'The parables of Jesus portray existential and ethical situations that are familiar to men yet are merely the point of departure for what the parables truly mean, that is, God's action vis-à-vis the world through the Son and the Spirit' (*TL2*: 79).

Following on from this, von Balthasar addresses this question from the other perspective, that of 'Negative theology', which starts from the insight that 'none of the things that surround us in this world can be what we seek, because all of them are finite and transitory and, therefore must be negated as such' (*TL2*: 90). While negative theology has long been a part of the Christian as well as philosophical tradition, the danger of what von Balthasar calls 'man's extra-biblical search for God' is that, 'weary of a seeking that never arrives at its goal', it 'takes refuge either in a system . . . or in a resigned agnosticism, which goes on negating even after it has already given up the quest' (*TL2*: 95). This is in contrast to that search for God which takes place 'in the light of the Bible' and instead sees the putting aside of earthly images, and even the 'annihilation' of the self, as rather 'the creation of space for God through the total surrender of all that is one's own'.

> Here 'negative theology' finally becomes the locus of perfect encounter, not in a dialogical equality of dignity, but in the transformation of the whole creature into an *ecce ancilla* [behold the handmaid] for the all-filling mystery of the ungraspable love of the self-emptying God. (*TL2*: 122)

In both of these sections, von Balthasar's approach is one which leans heavily on the concept of analogy, a concept which he has drawn from Przywara and interpreted in light of the teaching of the Fourth Lateran Council, of there being a 'similitude in "greater dissimilitude"' (*TL2*: 82) as regards human and divine logic and the creature's relationship to God. His explorations here lead him to conclude that the parables show perhaps more clearly than any other example, 'how divine logic can and will express itself in human logic on the basis of an *analogia linguae* [analogy of language] and, ultimately – in spite of all objections – an *analogia entis*, fulfilled in Christ, who is God and man in one person' (*TL2*: 81).

It is now time for von Balthasar to turn to a 'kata-logical' approach and the truth of the divine logic which 'comes down' to earth. But before doing this, he first has a chapter 'Logos and Logic in God' reflecting on the relationships and processions within the Trinity. This is important because of what he has already said about the triune life of God, and in this chapter he consciously draws on those sections addressing the same subject in *The Glory of the Lord* and *Theo-Drama*. His starting point is that there can be 'no access to the trinitarian mystery other than its revelation in Jesus Christ and the Holy Spirit' and that only 'Jesus' way of relating to his Father and to the Holy Spirit can teach us anything about the intratrinitarian relations of life and love in the one and only God' (*TL2*: 125). In Jesus is found that 'identity of unity and difference' (*TL2*: 128) which constitutes the divine life, which means that we can know by faith both that 'the hypostases really exist in their relative opposition' and that 'Father, Son and Holy Spirit are one God' (*TL2*: 133). He affirms once more, with Barth, that 'the economic Trinity, and it alone, reveals to us the immanent Trinity' (*TL2*: 138) and, in light of this understanding of the divine life, that 'the Son's mission (*missio*)' is to be understood as 'the continuation of his procession (*processio*) in the world' (*TL2*: 154). From this basis he can now plot the "kata-logical" path that 'descends from the Trinity to the world' (*TL2*: 169).

He begins with an account of the 'Trinitarian' and 'Ontological Difference', since for von Balthasar the difference between Creator and creation also has its roots in the Trinity. The relationship between the different persons of the Trinity provides for an understanding of difference which is not simply about distance and disobedience, but allows for the possibility of loving communication and inter-relationship. It is this freedom enjoyed within the Trinity which enables God freely to create a world which is other than himself, yet which is still capable of recognizing and responding to him.

> For how could worldly difference in its *maior dissimilitudo* with respect to the divine identity not ultimately be deemed a degradation, rather than something 'very good', if this difference did not have a root in God himself that was compatible with his identity? (*TL2*: 184)

It is thus a trinitarian understanding of being which allows for 'difference' to be seen as a 'positive reality' and for creation to be viewed as good, made by God, as Aquinas maintains 'for the sake of the love of his own goodness' (Quoted in *TL2*: 186).

We then turn to the final chapter, in which von Balthasar outlines his 'kata-logical' approach in three substantial sections; '*Verbum-Caro*' (the Word was made Flesh), '*Factum Est*' (It has 'taken place') and '*Caro Peccati*' (Flesh of Sin). In *Verbum-Caro* (*TL2*: 221–80) he addresses first the question as to why Jesus needed to become flesh, noting the different approaches to be found in the Bible, from the Old Testament and Wisdom accounts through to the Johannine and Pauline writings. His answer is that it is for two reasons which cannot be separated: 'First in order to restore what has been perverted and seduced from its end' and secondly because of God's merciful love and goodness, so that 'the ultimate reason is the predestination of the Son as the center and fulfilment of the universe' (*TL2*: 234). He then explores how Jesus uses the 'language of the flesh' in terms of such concepts as 'speech', 'myth', 'icon' and 'symbol', including a fascinating sub-section on 'metaphor' in which he reflects on Jüngel's attempt to 'ease the feud' between Barth and Przywara over the analogy of being (*TL2*: 273 note 109). The chapter closes with the reminder that to designate Jesus Christ as Word 'implies more than that he is mere discourse'. It is to say that he is a 'total "expression" of God, and in so doing to place the principal accent on the idea of "sovereign deed"' (*TL2*: 277).

The next section *Factum Est* establishes that this deed is something which has "taken place"; it is fact, indeed *the* fact and on 'the believing acceptance' of this one fact, 'the whole of theology stands or falls . . . ' (*TL2*: 281). However, the reception and interpretation of this fact must, for von Balthasar, involve the Church, 'the relevant criteria, even if they are made definitively effective by the Holy Spirit, must by their nature derive from the fact, from Christ as the Son of God, and must be fundamentally ecclesial'. This is due to the two factors which Christ has given 'directly to his Church in order to ensure the continued understanding of his message', namely 'communication in the truth' (by means of the Word and sacraments) and 'authority' (*TL2*: 282). From this starting point von Balthasar goes on to explore how this plays out in the story of Jesus' life and death, with particular reference to Adrienne von Speyr's writings on Jesus' birth, his 'vision and faith', and his dealing with 'freedom and temptation'.

However, this is not just about the life of Jesus on earth; it is also about the Son's sharing in the triune life of God. His mission is a work 'planned by the Trinity' with the Incarnation as its 'historical center' and the bestowal of the Holy Spirit as its 'eschatological consummation' (*TL2*: 296). As the 'Word made flesh', Jesus' life involves the whole of humanity which he came to save and redeem. And above all, it is a life which is shared by the Church, for the 'Church alone has an inward share in his life, death and Resurrection, both through baptism and the Eucharist, on the one hand, and through an existence lived in faith, on the other' (*TL2*: 308). Von Balthasar closes this section with a reflection on the enduring significance of the 'christological analogy' in light of these 'ana-' and 'kata-logical' approaches. His conclusion is that the 'original, always infinite, distance between God and creature' remains; what has changed is that now, 'within the recapitulation of the creature in Christ', it is not nullified but rather '*transfigured* into the infinite distance between the Divine Persons in the identity of the divine nature' (*TL2*: 315).

This leaves von Balthasar with the issue of human sinfulness and refusal to respond to God's word, and it is this subject he addresses in the final section *Caro Peccati*. In terms of logic, it is all about 'dialectic' since '*dia* means "apart", "asunder", so that contradiction, *dia-legein*, dialectic means the yawning abyss of sheer irreconcilability and enmity' (*TL2*: 317). This leads von Balthasar first into an exploration of the Biblical witness, and especially the theologies of John and Paul with their treatment of 'flesh' and 'spirit', from which he concludes they are 'free of every suspicion of introducing a dialectic, a necessary contradiction into Christian experience' in so far as this only the case 'where sinful man sets himself against' God and his providence (*TL2*: 334). He then goes on to engage in some detail with Luther's dialectical theology of the Cross. Von Balthasar's concern is that Luther's focus on the 'wrath-love contradiction of the Cross' (*TL2*: 342) leaves open the prospect of a 'naked God' standing outside and behind Christ's saving work. For von Balthasar, the key is to see the whole of salvation, even the dereliction of the Cross, as a drama involving the entire Trinity, and it is here once again that Adrienne von Speyr comes to the rescue. 'We ought to have the courage, according to Adrienne von Speyr, to interpret the mystery of hell's existence and inescapable finality within an *oikonomia* understood in trinitarian-christological terms' (*TL2*: 346). For her, ultimately, even hell is 'a trinitarian event' in that 'on Holy Saturday, the Son (as man and redeemer) is initiated into the dark mystery of the Father, which itself can happen only in secret and in silence' (*TL2*: 352). It is this mystery which prepares the way for Easter Sunday to be 'the victory of the triune God over every contradiction', as even death is 'swallowed up in victory' (*TL2*: 359).

5.3 *THE SPIRIT OF TRUTH*

A similar approach also marks the third and pneumatological volume of the *Theo-Logic. The Spirit of Truth* examines the role of the Holy Spirit both as the one who attests to the truth revealed in the Son and as the fulfilment of that truth, as humanity comes to share in the life of Christ through his body which is the Church. This volume begins with a series of 'Preludes' introducing themes which will re-emerge throughout the rest of the book. 'The Spirit's entire role is to guide us into the truth and to declare it: all the other, manifold utterances concerning the Spirit that we find in John and in the Scriptures of the Old and New Covenants come back to this fundamental role'. But the Spirit does not simply 'interpret a teaching', but also acts as a guide 'to the vital depths of what takes place between Father and Son'. Moreover, that 'space between Father and Son into which the Spirit introduces us, is in a certain respect the Spirit himself'. All of which means that, the Spirit is 'the love between Father and Son by being simultaneously their fruit and hence their witness' (*TL3*: 17–18).

However, for von Balthasar this trinitarian framework leads naturally to an ecclesial outcome, as the Spirit's declaration and leading into truth 'takes place pre-eminently in a particular realm that Paul calls the Body of Christ, or the Church'. It is here, 'effected essentially by the "Spirit of God" and the "Spirit of Christ" (Rom. 8:9), the Holy Spirit manifests himself as truth' (*TD3*: 19). This is not to say that the Spirit cannot also operate outside the Church, for this is a question to which von Balthasar will return later. But such a framework does show why the Spirit must have 'his inalienable place in *theo-logic*'. 'Christian truth is trinitarian because Jesus Christ, the Father's Son made man, incarnate through the Spirit and accompanied by the same Spirit through his life, work, and suffering, is the revealed Word and hence the "truth" (Jn 14:6) in that – unto death – he gives an adequate portrayal of the Father's love' (*TD3*: 23).

At the same time as introducing these themes, von Balthasar also asks two questions: first, whether it is possible to have a 'theology of the Spirit', which in light of the Patristic and New testament witness he answers firmly in the affirmative; and second, can there be a 'Spirit-Christology', to which he again answers yes, as will be evidenced in this volume. However, there are two interesting things about the way he formulates these answers: first that they involve an initial engagement with Hegel and his *Phenomenology of the Spirit*; and second that they lead him consciously to reflect on the experience of Barth, who wondered, at the end of his interpretation of Schleiermacher whether this theologian might not be better understood in terms of a theology of the Holy Spirit, and asked who might come after him to develop it.

What von Balthasar will seek to do in the last volume of his trilogy is to point towards what such a Catholic 'Spirit-Christology' might involve. He will do this in six substantial chapters, dealing in turn with the Spirit's role as 'Interpreter', then with 'the Holy Spirit as Person' (within the Trinity) which leads to a reflection on the Spirit as one of 'the Father's two hands'; then the following three chapters will engage with the Spirit's share in the 'Work of Salvation', the role of the 'Spirit and the Church' and the

'Spirit and World', before a final reflection on the way the Spirit points 'Onwards and Upwards to the Father'.

In the first of these chapters von Balthasar addresses the role of the Spirit as 'Interpreter' (*TL3*: 61–104) and characteristically begins by examining the Johannine witness in 'He will guide you into all the truth' (*TD3*: 69). Von Balthasar reflects on what John has to say in terms of 'making God known', of leading his disciples into 'all the Truth' and then in terms of the titles accorded to the Spirit, especially that of 'Paraclete'. At the same time, von Balthasar also notes that in John 'there is no particular statement about the link between it [theology] and the Holy Spirit; his entire work is an expression of it. From the earliest time he was called "the Theologian", which shows that what he has to say comes from the inner realm between Father and Son, inspired by the Spirit like no other writer' (*TD3*: 78). He then goes on to explore Paul's understanding of the Spirit, in particular 'the Spirit's function of interpreting the revelation in Christ' (*TD3*: 89), that of the rest of the New Testament, and even the Old Covenant, noting that the 'unity of God's Word and God's Spirit in the Old Covenant is of great significance in the context of our *theo-logical* task' (*TD3*: 99). The chapter then closes with a brief reference to how this subject is treated by the Fathers, which for von Balthasar is a pointer to the next subject, namely the 'personhood' of the Spirit or 'who' the Spirit is.

Characteristically, von Balthasar approaches this subject under four headings, engaging first with the Biblical witness ('What Scripture says') before exploring how it is dealt with by 'the Fathers', the theologians of the 'Middle Ages' and then of 'Modern Times', before pausing to see what has been clarified thus far. He notes the reticence with which the New Testament writers address this subject, reflecting the tension between the Spirit's being a 'divine reality located between God the Father and God the Son' while at the same time remaining 'elusive' and blowing where he wills. He also notes 'the unity and distinction between the Spirit filled Son . . . and the Holy Spirit' (*TL3*: 111) which leads to a further tension 'in the distinction, present in all the evangelists between the full presence of the Pneuma in the earthly Jesus and the outpouring of the Spirit upon the Church, or "upon all flesh" after his Resurrection and glorification . . . ' (*TL3*: 114). This reticence is also picked up by theologians of the patristic and mediaeval periods, whose work von Balthasar summarizes as follows:

> All Christian theology acknowledges that statements about the 'immanent' Trinity can only be reached via the 'economic' Trinity. The central achievement of the patristic period was to have demonstrated that the Spirit, on the basis of his 'economic' work as the Interpreter of Christ, in imparting genuinely divine gifts to men, must himself be God; the Fathers explicitly renounced the wish to clarify this divine and personal mode of being. Theology in the Middle Ages, following the same path from *oikonomia* to *theologia*, draws the implicit patristic insight into the full light of day: the *tropos hyparxeos* (mode of being) of the Divine Persons cannot be brought under any general concept, particularly since we cannot even conceptualise creaturely personhood. (*TL3*: 138)

Von Balthasar then explores how this subject was picked up in more recent times, noting first how the Reformers tended to a more restrictive approach, by 'fixing the Spirit upon the word of Scripture and the word of the Church' rather than the freedom allowed by the more traditional role of the Spirit as Interpreter (*TL3*: 148), before going on to look once more at the pneumatology of Hegel. He notes how Hegel's philosophy has its origins in theology, with an approach to the Church particularly influenced by the Pauline view of the 'Mystical Body of Christ in many members'. 'Theologically speaking, the ecclesial "objectivizations" (the word, understood as Scripture; sacrament; tradition; office) will be nothing other than forms fashioned by Christ's Holy Spirit in order to guide the subjective spirit of believers through the process of self-surrender towards that purity and universal expansion which it had always signified' (*TL3*: 154). Von Balthasar's conclusion from all this is that while 'the Trinity is and remains an absolute mystery' (*TL3*: 157) nevertheless, 'it is impossible to approach the Holy Spirit except from two sides, as the (subjective) epitome of the reciprocal love of Father and Son – whereby he appears as the bond (*nexus*) between them – and as the (objective) fruit that is produced by this love and attests it' (*TL3*: 160).

However, this still leaves open the question as to the relationship, or the processions, between the different Persons of the Trinity, and in particular the Son and the Spirit. This is the subject to which von Balthasar turns in his next chapter and its title, 'The Father's Two Hands', points to one of the key concepts which he will use. The concept of the 'Father's two hands' is one which von Balthasar draws from Irenaeus, and speaks of the way in which 'Son and Spirit proceed with equal directness from the Father' and equally are those 'with whose assistance he carries out the entire world project – from creation, via the redemption, to its final consummation in God' (*TL3*: 167). The other key concept is that of the 'trinitarian inversion' first outlined in the *Theo-Drama* (*TD3*: 183ff). This expresses the change in relationship between Spirit and Son, from the time of Jesus' earthly ministry when it was 'the Spirit of the Father and, hence, the Spirit of instruction from heaven' to the time of Christ's resurrection, when it is the Son who breathes his Spirit on his Church. But von Balthasar maintains that this 'economic' inversion

> changes nothing with respect to the *taxis* of the Divine Persons. What it does do, in accord with the theme of this section, is to point to the simultaneity of the missions of Son and Spirit, whose mutual relations change according to the needs of the *oikonomia*: first the Spirit is sent to incarnate the Son and accompany the man Jesus to his death; then, the Risen One can resume charge of the Spirit and, together with the Father, send him upon the Church. (*TL3*: 182)

It is the combination of these two themes which von Balthasar believes enables Christianity to answer the fundamental question facing all religions, namely how an historical person can aspire to universal validity, without denying the concrete existence of life or reducing it to a spiritual principle; 'it can only be solved along trinitarian or, more precisely, pneumatological lines. The Father works, not with one hand, but with both' (*TL3*: 196). Yet there still remains one matter to be resolved, namely the 'tiresome issue of the *filioque*' (*TL3*: 207) which remains a vexed subject between Eastern and Western Christians. Von Balthasar has already tried to show how the Spirit, in interpreting the two-fold movement both of the Father to the (incarnate) Son and that of the (risen) Son back to the Father, serves to draws together the Greek concept of 'divinisation' and the Latin concept of 'incorporation into Christ' so that 'on closer inspection the differences between these two concepts are almost entirely obliterated' (*TL3*: 186). But as regards the *filioque*, for all his even-handedness and willingness to share responsibility for the historical origins of the dispute, he remains firmly in support of the Western position as regards the outcome; namely that the Spirit proceeds from the Father and the Son. At the heart of this is his understanding of the Spirit as being both the 'epitome and fruit of the eternal love', a theme to be found throughout the New Testament, and one that leads not just him, but also Karl Barth 'to insist convincingly that this unity must be anchored in the immanent Trinity . . . ' (*TL3*: 218).

Von Balthasar's next task is to address 'The Role of the Spirit in the Work of Salvation' (*TL3*: 219–49). He does this in terms of 'three key words' which, he suggests, characterise the way 'the living God manifests himself in his mode of being as Holy Spirit', namely 'gift', 'freedom' and 'inward and outward testimony' (*TL3*: 223). *Gift* means 'what God hands over to man and puts within him', as 'God's love has been poured into our hearts through the Holy Spirit who has been given to us'" (Rom 5:5). *Freedom* is both a promise and a characteristic of the Christian life; 'Where the Spirit of the Lord is, there is freedom' (2 Cor. 3:17) but at the same time, as John reminds us, 'The wind blows where it will, and you hear the sound of it, but you do not know where it goes; so it is with everyone who is born of the Spirit' (Jn 3:8). *Testimony* is given by the Spirit both inwardly and outwardly. 'Outwardly he bears witness before the world, by convincing/convicting it (Jn 16:18ff.). Inwardly, 'the Spirit himself [bears] witness with our spirit that we are children of God' (Rom. 8:16)' (*TL3*: 223–4). Von Balthasar's aim in this chapter is to show 'that the three circles (gift, freedom, testimony) overlap and also that the concept "testimony" must include the notions of "interpreter" and "defender" (advocate)' (*TL3*: 249). However, his exploration of the role of testimony has already touched on another key arena, which is the role of the Spirit in the life of the Church, and it is this which will be the subject of his next chapter.

Von Balthasar's starting point in 'the Spirit and the Church' is that the Church exists for the sake of the world. 'Scripture nowhere says that God's plan is to redeem the Church; it is always a case of redeeming the world' (*TL3*: 255). But this mission of the Church is a two-fold movement which involves some risk.

> On the one hand the Church must go outward to the nations and teach them the Christian truth in such a way that they can understand and accept it ("inculturation"); and, on the other hand, she must take care that, with all its plurality, the truth does not become splintered; she must embrace it within her own "pleromatic" unity. (*TL3*: 259)

There remains, of course, the question as to when exactly the Church comes into being; is it in the covenant with Abraham or on Sinai; in the choice of the Disciples or the empowering of Pentecost? Von Balthasar maintains that 'what we mean by "Church" (in its distinctive sense) is present, in principle, as a result of the Incarnation of the Word, accomplished by the Spirit', and that although it is 'perfected on the Cross', it is the event of the Incarnation 'in which the "lowly" Maid, putting herself at heaven's disposal, is overshadowed by the Holy Spirit' which is 'the precondition for all that follows' (*TL3*: 283).

The universal 'work of world redemption' is one which involves both Son and Spirit; 'first came the work of the Passion of the Son through his bloody self-sacrifice "in the eternal Spirit" (Heb. 9:14)'. But it is a collaboration which also involves the Church, as this sacrifice is followed 'by the handing over of the Spirit by the Son, whereby he gave this Spirit, from the Father, to a Church speaking in a language that all peoples could understand, a Church that is sent out to all nations, to the ends of the earth' (*TL3*: 291). The Spirit then has a two-fold role in the economy of salvation in the Church and for the world; 'the Son gives the Spirit to the world both as "his" Spirit (the Spirit of obedience out of love for the Church . . .) and as the *trinitarian* gift that, henceforth, will be indistinguishably the Spirit of Father and Son and hence, can become the Church's unifying power' (*TL3*: 294). The gift of the Spirit at Pentecost will also point in two directions; 'toward the Church's missionary openness to the world and towards discipleship of Christ in persecution and death (understood as *martyrion*)' (*TL3*: 301).

This in turn leads von Balthasar to explore the work of the Spirit in terms of the distinction between the 'objective, institutional' and the 'subjective, existential element' in the life of the Church (*TL3*: 307). He maintains that both are necessary, and both are clearly seen in 'the two representative figures of the Church, that is Mary and Peter' (*TL3*: 312). Indeed, it is 'important to see not just *that*, but *how* the two aspects of the Church tend toward each other in order to become the one Church of Christ, both Body and Bride' and again to note that 'all objective holiness exists for the sake of the subjective movement of the Church's members towards the holiness of Christ in the Holy Spirit . . .' (*TL3*: 315). Furthermore he insists that 'the Holy Spirit is also responsible for the distinct existence, in Church office, of charismatic elements, on the one hand, and non-charismatic ecclesial charisms on the other' and that any tension between the two should 'be endured patiently, in the same Holy Spirit, in a spirit of ecclesial peace' (*TD3*: 317).

Having identified their common source, von Balthasar then has two long sections which explore first the 'objective' and the 'subjective' manifestations of the Spirit in the life of the Church. He deals with the 'objective' side in terms of the ecclesial structuring of the Church under the headings, 'Tradition-Scripture-Church Office', 'Proclamation and Liturgy', 'Sacraments' and (even) 'Canon Law', (for this 'arises simply from discipleship of Christ, in the same way that the Holy Spirit interprets the Spirit of Christ in the hearts of believers' (*TL3*: 354)). He then engages with the 'Subjective' side in terms of the life of Christian faith under the headings 'Spirit and Prayer', 'Forgiveness', 'Experience of the Spirit', 'Discernment of Spirits' and finally the 'Witness of Life'. His section on the 'Discernment of Spirits is particularly interesting because it is here that von Balthasar reflects on the modern 'charismatic movement', a movement about which he is somewhat cautious, not least because of what he perceives as its emphasis upon 'individual' gifting by the Spirit. 'Properly speaking, it is only the whole Church of Jesus Christ that is "charismatic", for in her every member has his gift from the Spirit. She alone, because of Christ's promise and gift, can boast of possessing (but not being able to manipulate) the Spirit . . .' (*TL3*: 399).

What has been offered here is just a short summary of a lengthy chapter running to some 160 pages. In contrast the chapter on 'Spirit and World' which follows amounts to a mere 15 pages. This contrast, as much as anything, serves to emphasize the strongly ecclesial nature of von Balthasar's pneumatology. He begins by reaffirming that the 'it is impossible to restrict the Spirit's sphere of activity to the realm of the Church' and that the Spirit 'impels, not only the Church to her perfection, but the world (which is in principle redeemed by Christ) as well'. This is because 'the nature of the world, even in its tiniest particles, seems to bear the stamp of its trinitarian origins' (*TL3*: 415–16). In this approach von Balthasar is following the lead of the Fathers, who 'most strongly emphasized the universal significance of the Incarnation of the Logos for the whole of mankind and for the whole cosmos' (*TL3*: 417). However, he is wary of more recent attempts at a doctrine of creation which speak of the Spirit as being somehow 'the Soul of the World' (as with Pannenberg and Teilhard de Chardin) in that they tend to diminish the role of Christ in God's saving drama. His closing reflection holds to this same emphasis. 'What is most creative about the Holy Spirit (*Creator Spiritus*) must be marked by the stigma of Cross and Resurrection as it spreads all over the world' (*TL3*: 429).

Von Balthasar's final chapter is a reflection on where the Spirit leads, which is 'the return, not only of Son and Spirit to the Father, but of the whole creation together with them and in them' (*TL3*: 433). This path of discipleship in Christ which leads to the Father 'goes simultaneously in two directions: vertically upward, and horizontally into the world in the proclamation of salvation to all nations and in the transformation of the world according to the Christian commandment of love' (*TL3*: 437). Moreover, it is not just a journey 'upward and onward' to the Father; it is also a journey deeper into the mystery of the Trinity, a mystery which has at its heart, 'the bold Johannine statement that "God is love"' (*TL3*: 445).

With this affirmation, von Balthasar feels able to confirm the validity of his approach as 'the concluding statements of the first volume of this *Theo-Logic*, which were formulated purely philosophically, are heightened and confirmed in a trinitarian context in the assertions of the second and third volumes' (*TL3*: 445). But it is not just the approach of the *Theo-Logic* alone; it is an affirmation of the trilogy as a whole. For von Balthasar's final reflection returns to the theme with which he began in *The Glory of the Lord*. 'What can it mean,' he asks, 'to "behold" the groundless abyss of love that the Father is?' How can we glimpse the glory of the invisible Father? In light of his exploration of the logic of divine love in the *Theo-Logic*, von Balthasar can now make his final answer. 'Through the Son's glory we glimpse the abyss of the invisible Father's love-glory in the Holy Spirit's twofold love. Born of the Spirit as we are, we exist in the fire of love in which Father and Son encounter each other; thus, together with the Spirit, we simultaneously bear witness and give glory to this love' (*TL3*: 448).

CHAPTER 6

RECEPTION AND FURTHER READING

6.1 *EPILOGUE*

Following the completion of his trilogy, von Balthasar published in 1987 a short work entitled *Epilogue*, written he maintained 'to afford the weary reader something like an overview of the whole enterprise' (*EP*: 9). The phrase 'something like' is important, because von Balthasar's intention is not to offer a 'digest' or summary of the arguments set out over the course of his great trilogy, but rather an explanation of why he has adopted his very distinctive approach, taking as his starting point not the fundamental doctrinal themes of Christian faith (the Trinity, christology, eschatology etc.) but instead the transcendentals of being, the beautiful, the good and the true.

This short book is set out in three parts, using the metaphor of a building or cathedral. In the 'forecourt' (or *Vorhalle*) we hear the claims not just of Christianity but of other religions and philosophies competing for adherents in the 'marketplace of religious wares'. But for von Balthasar, there remains an underlying question that modern positivist philosophies simply ignore, namely, what can be the meaning of a being whose essence is to ask after meanings? It is this question which suggests that 'being' is the central issue, and it leads him across the 'threshold' (or *Schwelle*). The key to his approach will be a simple one; 'whoever sees more of the truth, is more profoundly right' (*EP*: 15 & 43) and the three characteristics which bring out the fullness of being are its capacities for 'self-showing' (*Sich-zeigen*) for 'self-giving' (*Sich-geben*) and for 'self-saying' (*Sich-sagen*). It is these qualities lead naturally to an association with the beautiful, the good and the true, and in turn set the scene for his exposition of the *Aesthetics*, followed by the *Dramatics*, and concluding with the *Theo-Logic*.

They also establish a route for drawing together the questions raised by different religions and philosophies, thus enabling the enquirer to cross the threshold of faith and enter into the 'cathedral' (or *Dom*). There, in the inner sanctuary of Catholic Christian faith, will be found the 'sacred "public" *arcana* of Christian revelation' (*EP*: 89), the three inter-connected doctrinal themes at the heart of Christian faith: namely 'Christology and Trinity', 'The Word becomes Flesh' and 'Fruitfulness'.

Given our exploration of earlier volumes in the trilogy, the re-emergence of such subjects should come as no surprise. But in light of what we have said about the key influences on his work, it is significant that here again von Balthasar returns to the central themes which were at the heart of both what he learnt from Barth (namely the foundations for a christocentrism) and what he challenged in Barth (namely the inadequacy of his doctrine of the Church) and which led him to focus on the image of the vine and the theme of fruitfulness, a theme whose development in a Marian direction was strongly influenced by the writings of Adrienne von Speyr. And all of these are held together by that concept which von Balthasar learnt from Przywara, namely the analogy of being. 'This is possible only because all that is true in the world "hold[s] together" in him (Col. 1:17), which in turn presupposes that the *analogia entis* is personified in him, that he is the adequate sign, surrender, and expression of God within finite being' (*EP*: 89).

6.2 THE KEY INFLUENCES ON VON BALTHASAR

It is fascinating to see how in the *Epilogue* von Balthasar uses an architectural metaphor (in terms of a forecourt, threshold and sanctuary) to help articulate his theology. I have argued elsewhere (Wigley 2007) that it was von Balthasar's critical engagement with Barth which was to exercise just such a structural influence upon the development of his own theology; and that it was the debate over the analogy of being which led von Balthasar to re-affirm the centrality of ontology alongside revelation and to construct his own great trilogy in terms of the transcendentals of being.

However, while it can be argued that it was Barth whose influence was most significant in terms of shaping von Balthasar's trilogy, (and throughout this guide I have sought to keep in mind the structure of his argument – no mean task given the vast range of resources deployed across the 15 volumes) he is by no means the only colleague and theologian to have a substantial influence on von Balthasar's work. In Chapter 2, we identified four key influences on his trilogy, the impact of which we will now summarize.

The first was Henri de Lubac though whom von Balthasar rediscovered the richness of the Fathers. We have seen how Irenaeus' theme of the mutual glorification of humanity in God was to be a key theme not just in *The Glory of the Lord* but throughout the trilogy; how the role of human being in the saving drama is to be drawn into participation in the triune life of Father, Son and Holy Spirit, and thus to share in the life of God, (and in particular how this theme leads to the emergence of the Church as a theo-dramatic character in her own right). Moreover, this emphasis upon participation is not just one theme among many to be drawn from the Fathers; rather it is a pointer to that ongoing relationship, that conversation between theological companions, which is characteristic of von Balthasar's approach to the Fathers throughout the trilogy.

We have already mentioned the significance of Erich Przywara and the analogy of being. The role of analogy in understanding the relationship between God and creation, that sense of a greater dissimilarity within the similarity between the two which in turn points towards the tensions or 'polarities' in the human condition, and the role of Christ as the perfect analogy of being, the one who bridges and transcends the tensions which threaten human existence with disintegration, all these too are themes which run throughout the trilogy, right from the initial volume of the *Theo-Logic* to the 'Last Act' of the *Theo-Drama*. It is this analogical approach which von Balthasar learnt from Przywara, that he considers as an appropriate stance for a faith which wants to look outwards and engage with contemporary culture and philosophy, rather than hiding behind the bastions of Christian tradition.

Moreover, it was this argument over analogy which also framed his critical engagement with Karl Barth, the theologian from who he had learnt so much about the beauty and joy of God's revelation as he acknowledged in *The Glory of the Lord*. However, while picking up on Barth's highly christocentric approach, von Balthasar was also concerned about the 'constriction' or 'narrowing' in Barth's approach, in that everything was so accomplished in Christ that there was no place left for human response or engagement, and also about the inadequacy of Barth's doctrine of the Church. The *Theo-Drama* can thus be read as an 'opening up' of the space for human engagement in the drama of salvation, a space made possible by a christological interpretation of the analogy of being, so that the Christ-event is, as it were, extended into the life and faith of the Church which bears his name and is drawn to participate in his divine life, a participation which is the theme of the closing volumes of the *Theo-Logic*.

The last of these major influences was that of Adrienne von Speyr. There can be no doubt of the impact of her friendship on his life and work and we have noted how it was their joint commitment to the Community of St John forced von Balthasar to leave the Jesuit order. We have also suggested that his concern throughout *The Glory of the Lord* to reinstate the place of religious experience as part of the mainstream of Christian faith may have been influenced by the scepticism which greeted Adrienne's visions. However, it is in the last volumes of the *Theo-Drama* and then the *Theo-Logic* that her influence becomes more evident, as von Balthasar uses her mystical insights both to reflect on the depths of Christ' suffering on Holy Saturday, and also to show how this is part of the mystery of the Trinity, in terms of the love in letting go which characterizes the relationship between Father, Son and Holy Spirit.

6.3 RECEPTION OF VON BALTHASAR'S *TRILOGY*

In a work so comprehensive and encyclopaedic in outlook, it would be wrong to suggest that these were the only influences. Across the 15 volumes von Balthasar has, as we have seen, engaged with classical philosophers, mediaeval theologians and contemporary playwrights, revealing a breadth of interest and engagement which is difficult to keep up with, let alone summarize. However, there also emerges an intriguing relationship with another Jesuit colleague, Karl Rahner, which may serve as a helpful pointer to the way in which von Balthasar's work has been received in recent years. Rahner was a close contemporary of von Balthasar, a key figure in the reforms of the Second Vatican Council to which he was appointed as one of the official *periti* or theological experts, and founder of the theological journal *Concilium* in 1965, itself one of the major fruits of the Council.

We have already suggested that the first volume of von Balthasar's *Theo-Logic*, published in 1947 as *Wahrheit der Welt* or *Truth of the World*, can perhaps be read as a critical, though not unfriendly, response to Rahner's *Spirit in the World*. Von Balthasar continues to engage with Rahner in other volumes of his trilogy. In the *Theo-Drama*, for example, he is sympathetic to Rahner's linking together the economic and immanent Trinity, but highly critical of Rahner's treatment of soteriology and exposition of the relationship between the categorial and the transcendental, which for von Balthasar runs the risk of making Christ's atoning sacrifice just an extreme and explicit example of a more general and universal truth. In turn, this was to lead to his more outspoken criticism of Rahner's notion of 'anonymous Christianity' in his 1966 book, *Cordula oder der Ernstfall, The moment of Christian Witness*.

In the years following the Vatican Council, and as reaction set in against its reforms not just among traditional conservatives but from others who felt that too much of the riches of the past had been uncritically discarded without allowing for renewal from within, von Balthasar's stock started to rise. His initial works, such as his seminal study of Karl Barth had been of interest to ecumenical colleagues and scholars, but had been written at a time when he was on the margins and his own relationship with the Catholic Church under strain following his decision to leave the Jesuit order. Now the tide had started to turn. We have already noted Aidan Nichols' comment that, following the death of Adrienne and separated from the complications accompanying their relationship, 'he was exactly the kind of anti-liberal but reforming theologian, neo-patristic in his sympathies, with whom the Roman see in the later years of Paul VI's pontificate and that of John Paul II like to do business' (Nichols 2000: xix). The change in his standing is reflected in Von Balthasar's appointment to the Pope's International Theological Commission in 1969, his friendship with Cardinal Ratzinger and their establishing of a rival theological journal, *Communio*, in 1972.

This development is also noted by another commentator on Catholic affairs, John L. Allen Jnr., who suggests that 'the basic options in Roman Catholic theology after the second Vatican Council (1962–1965) can be expressed in terms of a choice between two German-speaking sons of Ignatius Loyola: Karl

Rahner and Hans Urs von Balthasar'. Moreover, Allen continues, 'if the Rahnerians held the upper hand for the first 20 years, the Balthasarians dominate today, at least in terms of official church policy' (*National Catholic Reporter*, 28 November 2003). Moreover, at Von Balthasar's funeral in 1988, it was Cardinal Ratzinger (later to be elected Pope Benedict XVI) who gave the eulogy, and who received a telegram from Pope Paul VI describing von Balthasar as 'a great son of the Church, an outstanding man of theology and of the arts, who deserves a special place of honour in contemporary ecclesiastical and cultural life' (Quoted in David L. Schindler (ed.) 1991: 289).

Such statements are not merely a summary of contemporary theological trends or politics; there is a deeper meaning and substance behind them. What von Balthasar's trilogy offered the Vatican was three things; first a creative reinterpretation of the Church Fathers and the Catholic tradition, including the works of Anselm and Aquinas, which took that broad sweep of history and brought it into a living relationship with the contemporary situation; secondly an engagement not just with the biblical and christocentric focus of Protestant scholars like Barth but also the insights of Western culture and philosophy, and yet which ended up with a theology that remained thoroughly trinitarian and ecclesial; and thirdly, within this broadly ecumenical approach, von Balthasar arrived at an ecclesiology in which the teaching office and authority of the Church was not merely preserved but actually enhanced. For, as we saw in the *Theo-Drama*, von Balthasar's conviction is that, 'Christ only exists together with the community of saints united in the *Immaculata*, together with the communion of the ministerial office visibly united in Peter and his successors and together with the living, ongoing tradition united in the great councils and declarations of the Church' (*TD4*: 456).

It would be inadequate to describe von Balthasar's theology as simply a new way to restate old claims to authority, although as Nichols also points out, it 'did no harm that von Balthasar's book on *The Office of Peter and the Structure of the Church* is theologically the profoundest book on the papacy ever written' (Nichols 2000: xix). Instead, and partly mirroring the experience of his own ministry and commitment to the Community of St John, von Balthasar found his own unique way to hold together the distinctive but complementary witnesses of St John and St Peter, in a theology where the charismatic and the institutional both have their proper part to play in serving the life and mission of the Church.

However, von Balthasar's trilogy has not just been influential among Catholic circles, it has also had a wider impact on current theology, and in two areas in particular. In the first place his work has contributed to a revival of interest in Christian aesthetics, the idea that Christian theology should not just be concerned with the relevance of the Gospel message to contemporary needs and situations, but is first and foremost an encounter with the beauty and glory of God in Jesus Christ, an encounter in which human beings are caught up in wonder, love and praise and through though which they are transformed and made capable of transforming the world. These themes are part of what von Balthasar found in his relationship with Karl Barth (and shared in their mutual enjoyment of Mozart) and von Balthasar's work, especially *The Glory of the Lord*, will be a major reference point in works of theologians coming from such different perspectives as the Anglican, Richard Harries (in *Art and the Beauty of God*), the Catholic, Aidan Nichols (in *Christendom Awake – On Re-energising the Church in Culture*, and the Orthodox, David Bentley Hart (in *The Beauty of the Infinite*).

Two other recent studies may serve also to make the point. Richard Viladesau prefaces his *Theological Aesthetics* by observing that, 'A study of this kind could hardly fail to take into account the monumental *Theological Aesthetics* of Hans Urs von Balthasar' (Viladesau 1999: ix). Similarly Patrick Sherry's introduction to the subject, *Spirit and Beauty*, begins by acknowledging that von Balthasar is 'perhaps the greatest modern writer on theological aesthetics' (Sherry 2002: 15) and among theologians one of the few for whom aesthetics is a theme right at the centre of their theology, as evidenced in *The Glory of the Lord*.

A second area where von Balthasar's trilogy has contributed to current theological debate is in the attempts of theologians to address postmodern concerns about 'truth' and 'difference'. Von Balthasar's detailed discussion of the relationships between the Divine Persons, within a firmly trinitarian account of the *Theo-Drama*, is significant in this because he identifies the origins of 'difference' within the triune relationship of 'love' and 'letting go' in God. It is the loving relationships between Father, Son and

Holy Spirit which make it possible for distance to be seen as something other than alienation and separation (and in turn make it possible for the existence of a creation which can freely respond to its Creator). This is a theme which has been picked up in a recent collection of essays *Balthasar at the End of Modernity* (eds. Gardner, Moss, Quash and Ward) and is also very much at the forefront of David Schindler's recent study, *Hans Urs von Balthasar and the Dramatic Structure of Truth*, in which he explores how 'the resources provided by von Balthasar open up another possibility, one that takes full account of difference *as a matter of truth and reason* itself' (Schindler 2004: 2).

However, all this it not to say that von Balthasar's work has been received uncritically. There are perhaps three major areas of concern expressed which are worth noting. The first follows on from what we have said earlier in this section and reflects of the role of Church in von Balthasar's theology. We have noted already that this was an ongoing issue in his relationship with Barth, and it is significant that in the later volumes of his *Dogmatics* Barth repeated his concern that the welcome return to a christocentric focus found in von Balthasar should not be obscured by too much attention being paid to the lives of his saints *(CDIV.1*: 768). This is a concern which has been picked up in more detail by Ben Quash in his recent study *Theology and the Drama of History*. Quash raises the question as to whether there is a too 'harmonious resolution' in the outworking of the mission of Christ in the life of the Church, and whether this leads to a more static and institutional model of Church than should be envisaged in a genuinely dramatic encounter. His conclusion is that a 'tendency to impose resolution represents a serious undercutting of the effectiveness of von Balthasar's use of analogy' and that 'the doctrine of the Church suffers in this way because a debilitated doctrine of analogy allows it to' (Quash 2005: 192).

The second follows on from this and is the concern as to how far von Balthasar engages with the idea of a social reality outside the Church; in particular whether he is interested in the engagement of Christians with the wider world. This is a concern raised by Gerard O'Hanlon in an article on the 'Theological Dramatics' (in *The Beauty of Christ*, Eds. McGregor and Norris, 1994). O'Hanlon notes the caution with which von Balthasar engages with liberation theology in Volume IV of the *Theo-Drama* and his warning against 'a utopian approach to hope for a better world that has more in common with Marx and Hegel than with the Christian gospel' (McGregor and Norris, 1994: 104). But at the same time, O'Hanlon notes the absence in the *Theo-Drama* of 'any great sense of drama, of passionate engagement in the project for a new world order', something which is accompanied by 'almost a detached neutral stance . . . to structures such as capitalism and patriarchy which is naïve rather than merely politically innocent' and 'arguably an over sanguine view taken of the ability of the Church to mirror more closely than civil society the Kingdom of God in her own conduct and structures'. What is needed to correct this, suggests O'Hanlon, and to build on the useful but critical comments which von Balthasar makes in terms of social theology, is 'a development of Balthasar beyond himself, using his magnificent trilogy, and in particular the Theo-Drama, to articulate a more historical engagement of God with human reality' (McGregor and Norris, 1994: 107–10).

Linked to this is von Balthasar's approach to anthropology and in particular the implications of his insistence on the fundamental polarity of sexual difference. This is an issue picked up in Corinne Crammer's essay in *The Cambridge Companion to Hans Urs von Balthasar*. (eds. Oakes and Moss, 2004) While a renewed emphasis on sexual differentiation is not something dismissed by all feminist theologians, von Balthasar's particular views on the feminine aspect, one characterized by acceptance and obedience and reflected in the distinctive Marian shape adopted in his theology, is not one which is universally accepted. Crammer rightly points out that it leads not just to a traditional approach to women's role in society but also, when contrasted with the proposal of such key masculine characteristics as leadership, to an understanding of women's role in the Church which is highly conservative and clearly opposed to any campaign for women's ordination. Her conclusion is that 'Balthasar's theology of the sexes is likely to arouse a strong reaction from those concerned with issues of social justice and equal rights for women . . . Whatever his intentions may have been, Balthasar's theology does not serve the cause of justice for women well but rather provides theological justification for social inequality' (Oakes and Moss, 2004: 107).

The final point of concern is one which von Balthasar himself acknowledges right at the beginning of the trilogy, when he ends the foreword to the first volume of his *Theological Aesthetics* by saying, 'The overall scope of the present work naturally remains all too Mediterranean. The inclusion of other cultures, especially that of Asia, would have been important and fruitful. But the author's education has not allowed for such an expansion . . .' (*GL1*: 11). Von Balthasar's trilogy is a massive and encyclopaedic undertaking, but it is one which deals essentially with the integration of Western culture and Christianity. Without undermining von Balthasar's achievement, there remains the question as to how far it engages with a Christian faith which is now global, increasingly composed of adherents from outside mainland Europe and its Classical tradition, and having to engage more fully with the huge variety of other cultures and religions to be found around and increasingly across the world.

This becomes a particular issue given the strongly ecclesial nature of von Balthasar's theology and the normative role he ascribes to the archetypal experience of Mary and the Apostles in shaping the institutional structure of the Church. In light of the changing make up and geographical dynamics of the Catholic Church, as in other Christian traditions, with a decline in Europe contrasted with areas of rapid growth in Asia and Africa, there must remain a question as to how far this very European and twentieth-century narrative can serve to interpret the Church in a twenty-first century and global context, especially where she has to address the issues of global debt, climate change and the re-emergence of international conflicts which have at least in part a religious causation. These are all part of the challenge which his friend and former colleague, now Pope Benedict XVI is currently having to face as leader of the Catholic Church. Perhaps all that we can do here is to recognize that however substantial von Balthasar's achievement in the trilogy, the work is not complete, and to note the final words in his Foreword; 'May those qualified come to complete the present fragment' (*GL1*: 11).

6.4 FURTHER READING OF VON BALTHASAR

Notwithstanding the efforts of this guide, it will not be surprising if some readers find the 15 volumes of von Balthasar's trilogy too forbidding a task to start with. In light of this, we here offer a pointer to four of his shorter works which may help to provide a way into his theology.

The Theology of Karl Barth

We have already written about the significance of Karl Barth for the development of von Balthasar's theology (and have argued elsewhere that it is his engagement with Barth over the analogy of being which serves as the key influence on the structure of von Balthasar's trilogy). However, this seminal study of Barth's theology first published in 1951 is still worth reading on its own account. In the first place it is a hugely insightful reading of Barth's theology, one which has had a major influence on the interpretation of Barth (for all that von Balthasar's thesis of a conversion from 'dialectic' to 'analogy' over the course of Barth's development from his commentary on Romans to the mature volumes of his *Church Dogmatics* has recently been challenged by McCormack and others). It is an interpretation which, characteristically of von Balthasar, and indeed of Barth, draws on a wide gallery of other theological perspectives across the centuries from Augustine to Aquinas and from the Scholastics to Schleiermacher.

It is also a study which was noted, and to some extent approved, by Barth himself. But von Balthasar's work was about more than mere interpretation, for in expounding on Barth von Balthasar found himself engaging with a theologian who, in addition to rediscovering the beauty and wonder of God's revelation, had also raised up the most profound challenge to Catholic theology, a challenge to which von Balthasar felt himself honour bound to respond. Accordingly, the second half of his study finds von Balthasar explicitly offering a Catholic response to the challenges which Barth had raised on various subjects, for example, on 'Christ and Creation', 'Nature and History', 'Judgement and Redemption', 'Grace and Sin'.

Moreover, in the course of doing this, von Balthasar came to see more clearly which of Barth's insights were those that 'ought to be given serious consideration by Catholic theology'. For von Balthasar, the key ones were as follows: 'those that involve the foundations for a christocentrism, for the historicity of nature and the created character of worldly truth' (*KB*: 383). It was just these concerns which, as we have suggested, were to become themes which run through the whole of von Balthasar's trilogy, alongside his intent to reclaim a christological basis for the analogy of being and his concern to resist that Christological 'constriction' or 'narrowing' he found in Barth and provide an appropriate space for human response to God's gracious invitation in Christ. In all this, we find von Balthasar pointing towards that understanding of a redemption which 'comes to us respecting our incarnate lives in time, leaving room for us to continue to change as we follow in the footsteps of the incarnate Lord' (*KB*: 378). And all this leads to that call to participate in God's great act of salvation which is the theme of von Balthasar's *Theo-Drama*.

Love Alone: The Way of Revelation

This short work comprising just over a hundred pages was written in 1963, shortly after the publication of the first three volumes of *The Glory of the Lord*. It is intended, as von Balthasar himself points out, as a 'sketch' which will 'follow the basic pattern' of the larger work, providing a 'theological aesthetic in the dual sense of a study of perception, and a study of the objective self-expression of the divine glory'. Von Balthasar's starting point is that 'Christian self-understanding (and so theology) is found neither in a wisdom superior to that of the world's religions, based on divine information . . . nor on the definitive fulfilment of man as a personal and social being through the realization of the effects of a revelation and redemption . . . but solely in the self-glorification of Divine love: *ad maiorem Divini Amoris GLORIAM*' (*LA*: 8).

In this little book, von Balthasar explores initially the failure of the 'Cosmological method' which seeks to ground the Christian faith on the basis of an understanding of the world, and then of the 'Anthropological Method' which seeks to ground it on an understanding of human being. The answer, for von Balthasar, is a third way, the 'Way of Love', in which 'the form of Christian revelation is seen as wholly that of the glorification of divine love' (*LA*: 50). Von Balthasar then explores what this means in terms of Love, understood in turn as 'Revelation', as 'Justification', as 'Deed', and as 'Form' (in the process introducing some of the themes which will be expanded in much greater detail in the volumes of his trilogy) before ending with a section on 'Love as the Light of the World'.

His conclusion is that Logos, that reason which comprehends everything, 'can only be found in revelation itself' that comes from God and provides the centre around which everything can be grouped' (*LA*: 119). This cannot be understood simply in terms of the traditional Catholic sense of a multiplicity of dogma, nor in the Protestant way of obedience to a self-authenticating word of Scripture. What they both need is to be conformed to the glory of God's love revealed in Jesus Christ, for only in light of a 'twofold loving obedience to Church and to Scripture does the "doctrine" of a loving God appear relevantly and convincingly as the mystery of love perpetuated in the here and now' (*LA*: 121).

First Glance at Adrienne von Speyr

This book is von Balthasar's tribute to Adrienne's life and work and was published in 1968, the year after her death on the feast day of St Hildegard, 17 September 1967. It is written in three parts: the first is von Balthasar's account of her life (and this includes her upbringing, medical career, conversion to the Catholic faith, increasing physical sufferings and accompanying mystical experiences) her theological insights and her works; the second, a selection of statements in which she reflects on her own life and faith; and the third a selection of her prayers. We have already explored the influence of Adrienne on von Balthasar's life and ministry in our second chapter. The interest of this book is that it reveals in von Balthasar's own words his own sense of indebtedness to her for his own theology and for the direction it took in his trilogy.

It is in part an acknowledgement of that debt, and in part a claim to have her mission and her religious experience rehabilitated into the mainstream of a Catholic Church which had been all too suspicious of those spiritual gifts during her life-time. Accordingly, von Balthasar ends his foreword as follows:

> As her confessor and spiritual director, I observed her interior life most closely, yet in twenty-seven years I never had the least doubt about the authentic mission that was hers, nor about the unpretentious integrity with which she lived it and communicated it to me. I not only made some of the most difficult decisions in my life – including my decision to leave the Jesuit Order – following her advice, but I also strove to

bring my way of looking at Christian revelation into conformity with her. If it had been otherwise, many an article in *Essays in Theology* and, especially, the basic perspective of *Herrlichkeit* would never have existed (though Adrienne had not the least part in their actual composition). (*FG*: 12)

Mysterium Paschale: The Mystery of Easter

This more substantial work, first published in 1970, is a characteristic example of the way in which von Balthasar's writing weaves together the threads of material which is at the same time theological, devotional and even liturgical. Its concern is to explore the mystery of the Christ's passion as it is unfolds in the three days of the Easter story. But within his account is revealed some of the key themes which we have found elsewhere in von Balthasar's theology, namely the concern to relate 'the event of the Kenosis of the Son of God to what one can, by analogy, designate as the eternal "event" of the divine processions' (*MP*: viii), or how to account for the suffering death of Christ on the Cross within a theological framework that is fully trinitarian.

Von Balthasar does this in five chapters which engage fully with the Biblical material, the witness of the Fathers, the insights of contemporary theologians and the mystical experiences of his colleague Adrienne von Speyr. The first chapter addresses the relationship between Christ's Incarnation and Passion, and surveys the 'entire economy of salvation' with a view to reveal 'the Incarnation as ordered to the Passion'. The second explores the 'Death of God' in terms of that ultimate Kenosis or self-emptying of God which both embodies and then overcomes the difference between a *theologia crucis* and a *theologia gloriae*. The last three chapters then offer von Balthasar's account of the three days of Easter, engaging in turn with 'Going to the Cross: Good Friday', 'Going to the Dead: Holy Saturday' and finally 'Going to the Father: Easter', and of these it is his account of 'Holy Saturday', Christ's entering into and liberation from Hell which has drawn most theological interest and attention.

However, such an outline offers only the bare bones of von Balthasar's account; it is a deeper reading of particular episodes that shows how his theological imagination engages creatively with the Easter story. An example is his richly allegorical account of what happens in John's Gospel when Peter and the Beloved

Disciple both run together to the empty Tomb, and how it is that
the Beloved Disciple, arriving first (since 'love is unencumbered
by office') nevertheless stops to allow Peter to enter the Tomb
first. For von Balthasar all this 'suggests a Church with two
poles: the Church of office and the Church of love, with a harmonious tension between them, the official function working for
love, love respectively allowing first place to office' (*MP*: 259).
It is just such a 'harmonious tension' which may be said to characterize von Balthasar's own relationship with the Church during
the long and sometimes complex course of his ministry.

Moreover, all these different threads and themes of his writing,
the theological, devotional and the liturgical are drawn together
in the closing words of his preface to the second edition.

> God then, has no need to 'change' when he makes a reality of
> the wonders of his charity, wonders which include the Incar-
> nation and, more particularly, the Passion of Christ, and,
> before him, the dramatic history of God with Israel and, no
> doubt, with humanity as whole. All the contingent 'abase-
> ments' of God in the economy of salvation are forever included
> and outstripped in the eternal event of Love. And so what, in
> the temporal economy, appears as the (most real) suffering on
> the Cross is only the manifestation of the (Trinitarian) Eucha-
> rist of the Son: he will be forever the slain Lamb, on the throne
> of the Father's glory, and his Eucharist – the Body shared out,
> the Blood poured forth – will never be abolished, since the
> Eucharist it is which must gather all creation into his body.
> What the Father has given, he will never take back. (*MP*: ix)

6.5 FURTHER READING ABOUT VON BALTHASAR
General Introductions

The amount of secondary material on von Balthasar has grown
enormously in recent years. However, Edward T. Oakes' study,
originally published in 1994, *Pattern of Redemption: The Theology of Hans Urs von Balthasar*, remains perhaps the most
accessible and informative introduction to von Balthasar's theology. Oakes was the translator of von Balthasar's *The Theology
of Karl Barth*, and his book is particularly helpful in drawing out
the intellectual background to von Balthasar's theology and

those sources which most influenced his trilogy. Oakes has also co-edited, with David Moss, the *Cambridge Companion to Hans Urs von Balthasar* (2004) and this volume has a number of interesting and introductory essays dealing in turn with 'Theological Topics' (themes in his theology), 'the Trilogy' (the works themselves, 'Disciplines' (his theological approach) and 'Contemporary Encounters' (his engagement with other theologians), some of which we have already referred to in this guide.

The most recent introduction to von Balthasar is Rodney Howsare's *Balthasar, a Guide for the Perplexed* (2009). After the opening chapters which set his life and work in context and then address his 'Theological Style', this study offers a more thematic introduction to von Balthasar's theology, dealing with 'Jesus Christ' and in turn 'the Meaning of Scripture', 'the Drama of Finite and Infinite Freedom' and then 'the Trinity and the Cross', all themes which we have noted earlier. There are two things which Howsare shares in common with this guide, in that he too recognizes the sometimes 'perplexing' aspect of von Balthasar's theology and that his introduction to his life and work identifies the same key influences as being in turn Erich Przywara, Henri de Lubac, Adrienne von Speyr and Karl Barth. An older, but still serviceable Introduction from a more traditional Catholic perspective is John O'Donnell's volume in the 'Outstanding Christian Thinkers' series published in 1991.

Another very helpful resource, although not strictly an introduction, is the collection edited by David L. Schindler *Hans Urs von Balthasar* (1991). In the absence of a full-blown biography, this volume contains a very useful 'Sketch of his Life' by his cousin, Peter Henrici, as well as 'A Résumé of My Thought' written by von Balthasar himself and originally published in *Communio* in 1988, just before his death.

Introductions to the *Trilogy*

The most comprehensive introduction to the trilogy is Aidan Nichols' three volume work, *The Word has been abroad: a Guide through Balthasar's Aesthetics* (1998), *No Bloodless Myth: a Guide through Balthasar's Dramatics* (2000), and *Say it is Pentecost: a Guide through Balthasar's Logic* (2001). Nichols is an extremely well informed and educated commentator, particularly on the Catholic background to von Balthasar's theology, and has also written introductions to other volumes of von Balthasar's work. His three volume guide, running to some nearly nine hundred pages, amounts to a substantial work in is own right, even if it can sometimes read more like a commentary than an introduction.

There are two other collections of essays which also serve to introduce the trilogy. The first, and perhaps the better of the two, is *The Analogy of Beauty* edited by John Riches (1986). It originated in a tribute to celebrate von Balthasar's 80th birthday and includes essays from a number of scholars who contributed to the translation of *The Glory of the Lord*, as well as two very revealing assessments by von Balthasar himself of his own work 'In Retrospect' and after 'Another Ten Years – 1975'. The second collection, *The Beauty of Christ* edited by Bede McGregor and Thomas Norris (1994), grew out of a 1992 Conference seeking to explore the impact of his theology in terms of 'Christ, Beauty, and the Third Millennium'. As a collection of papers, it is perhaps a more of a mixed bag with essays which range from the critical to the more hagiographical; however it does deal with a broader range of themes across the trilogy, rather than the Riches' collection which concentrates more on the *Theological Aesthetics.*

Specific Aspects of the *Trilogy*

As we have mentioned earlier, the volume of secondary literature on Von Balthasar is growing rapidly. In terms of specific aspects of his theology, W. T. Dickens' *Hans Urs von Balthasar's Theological Aesthetics: a Model for Post-Critical Biblical Interpretation* (2003) explores the hermeneutical approach which underlies his approach to the Bible, especially in the Aesthetics. Dickens particularly focuses on von Balthasar's concern not simply to dismiss modern critical methods but to pay more attention to the traditional idea of the *sensus fidelium* and to Patristic understandings of Scripture, as being not just normative for the Church but also in some way representative of the Body of Christ.

Other significant studies are those on *The Immutability of God in the Theology of Hans Urs von Balthasar* by Gerard O'Hanlon (1990) and *The Dramatic Encounter of Divine and Human Freedom in the Theology of Hans Urs von Balthasar* by Thomas Dalzell (2000), both of which themes, divine immutability and the encounter of divine and human freedom, we have found to have a key role to play in von Balthasar's *Theo-Drama* especially. Ben Quash's *Theology and the Drama of History* (2005) is another study to engage seriously with the *Theo-Drama* and with von Balthasar's reading of both history and literature. His conclusions are quite challenging in terms of von Balthasar's doctrine of the Church, and not least because of his understanding of von Balthasar's previous engagement with Przywara and Barth as well as von Balthasar's reading of Hegel and Manley Hopkins. Following on, and to a degree overlapping both the *Theo-Drama* and the *Theo-Logic*, is D. C. Schindler's book, *Hans Urs von Balthasar and the Dramatic Structure of Truth: a Philosophical Investigation* (2004). This is a serious and complex study of von Balthasar's engagement with modern philosophy which seeks to show how a relational (and dramatic) approach, that takes seriously the idea of mystery and difference, offers a more complete way to understand the fullness of truth.

There are also studies which have engaged with von Balthasar's style of theology. From a distinctively Catholic perspective, there is the short but profound book by his friend and colleague Angelo Scola, *Hans Urs von Balthasar: A Theological Style* (1995) which reflects on his theology after the manner of von Balthasar's own 'Studies in theological style' in Volumes II and III of his Aesthetics. In contrast, there is also Rodney Howsare's more recent study, *Hans Urs von Balthasar and Protestantism: the Ecumenical Implications of his Theological Style* (2005) which explores von Balthasar's theology in terms of his dialogue with two central figures of Protestant theology, namely Martin Luther and Karl Barth, as well as with different approaches within his own Catholic tradition, for example Karl Rahner.

Finally there are studies which explore the different sources and influences on von Balthasar's trilogy. We have already mentioned the influence of de Lubac and his reading of Irenaeus in particular. Kevin Mongrain's *The Systematic Thought of Hans Urs von Balthasar: an Irenaean Retrieval* (2002) is an attempt to make this the dominant structural influence on the trilogy, an attempt which, though not without some credibility, is perhaps overstated. Another, much earlier, study which aims to draw out the Patristic sources of *The Glory of the Lord* in particular is Louis Robert's *The Theological Aesthetics of Hans Urs von*

Balthasar (1987) while Mark McIntosh's more recent study, *Christology from Within: Spirituality and the Incarnation in Hans Urs von Balthasar* (2000) seeks to interpret von Balthasar by means of a Patristic reading of Christology (especially that of Maximus the Confessor) combined with an Ignatian reading of spirituality.

However, while it can not be disputed that the range of interests and influences on von Balthasar's theology is vast, as indeed this guide has indicated, I still remain of the opinion that the most helpful way to read the trilogy and to see how the structure of his argument develops, is through the lens of his engagement and sustained argument with Karl Barth over the 'analogy of being' formulated by his mentor, Erich Przywara. It is this approach which I outlined in the previously mentioned study, *Karl Barth and Hans Urs von Balthasar: A Critical Engagement* (2007) and, notwithstanding all the other arguments made above, I consider that such an approach still has much to recommend it.

NOTES

CHAPTER 1

1. In the absence of a full scale biography of von Balthasar, this short account of his life will draw heavily on 'Hans Urs von Balthasar: A Sketch of His Life' by his cousin Peter Henrici, S. J. published in David L. Schindler, (ed.), *Hans Urs von Balthasar: His Life and Work* (San Francisco Ignatius Press, 1991) pp. 7–43

CHAPTER 2

1. Henri de Lubac S.J., 'A Witness of Christ in the Church: Hans Urs von Balthasar' in David L. Schindler (ed.), *Hans Urs von Balthasar: His Life and Work* (San Francisco: Ignatius Press, 1991) pp. 272–73
2. 'In Retrospect' in John Riches (ed.), *The Analogy of Beauty: The Theology of Hans Urs von Balthasar* (Edinburgh: T&T Clark:1986) pp. 194–221; originally *Rechenschaft* (Einsiedeln: Johannes Verlag, 1965)
3. McCormack, Bruce L., *Karl Barth's Critically Realistic Dialectical Theology: Its Genesis and Development 1909–1936* (Oxford: Clarendon Press, 1995)
4. *First Glance at Adrienne von Speyr* tr. Antje Lawry and Sergia Englund, O.C.D., (San Francisco: Ignatius Press, 1981) originally *Erster Blick auf Adrienne von Speyr* (Einsiedeln: Johannes Verlag, 1968)

BIBLIOGRAPHY

PRIMARY SOURCES

1. The Trilogy

Herrlichkeit: Eine theologische Ästhetik (Einsiedeln: Johannes Verlag, 1961–69)
ET *The Glory of the Lord: A Theological Aesthetics* (Edinburgh: T&T Clark, 1982–89)

Volume I: *Seeing the Form*, tr. Erasmo Leivà-Merikakis (Edinburgh: T&T Clark, and San Francisco: Ignatius Press, 1982)
Volume II: *Studies in Theological Style: Clerical Styles*, trs Andrew Louth, Francis McDonagh and Brian McNeil (Edinburgh: T&T Clark, and San Francisco: Ignatius Press, 1984)
Volume III: *Studies in Theological Style: Lay Styles*, trs Andrew Louth, John Saward, Martin Simon, and Rowan Williams (Edinburgh: T&T Clark, and San Francisco: Ignatius Press, 1986)
Volume IV: *In the Realm of Metaphysics in Antiquity*, trs Brian McNeil, Andrew Louth, John Saward, Rowan Williams, and Oliver Davies (Edinburgh: T&T Clark, & San Francisco: Ignatius Press, 1989)
Volume V: *In the Realm of Metaphysics in the Modern Age*, trs Oliver Davies, Andrew Louth, Brian McNeil, John Saward, and Rowan Williams (Edinburgh: T&T Clark, & San Francisco: Ignatius Press, 1991)
Volume VI: *Theology: The Old Covenant*, trs Brian McNeil and Erasmo Leivà-Merikakis (Edinburgh: T&T Clark, and San Francisco: Ignatius Press, 1991)
Volume VII: *Theology: The New Covenant*, tr. Brian McNeil (Edinburgh: T&T Clark, & San Francisco: Ignatius Press, 1989)

Theodramatik (Einsiedeln: Johannes Verlag, 1973–83)
ET *Theo-Drama: Theological Dramatic Theory* (San Francisco: Ignatius Press,1988–98)

Volume I: *Prolegomena*, tr. Graham Harrison (San Francisco: Ignatius Press, 1988)
Volume II: *Dramatic Personae: Man in God*, tr. Graham Harrison (San Francisco: Ignatius Press, 1990)
Volume III: *Dramatis Personae: Persons in Christ*, tr. Graham Harrison (San Francisco: Ignatius Press, 1992)
Volume IV: *The Action*, tr. Graham Harrison (San Francisco: Ignatius Press, 1994)

Volume V: *The Final Act*, tr. Graham Harrison (San Francisco: Ignatius Press, 1998)

Theologik (Einsiedeln: Johannes Verlag, 1985–87)
ET *Theo-Logic* (San Francisco: Ignatius Press, 2000–05)

Volume I: *Truth of the World*, tr. Adrian J. Walker (San Francisco: Ignatius Press, 2000)
Volume II: *Truth of God*, tr. Adrian J. Walker (San Francisco: Ignatius Press, 2004)
Volume III: *The Spirit of Truth,* tr. Adrian J. Walker (San Francisco: Ignatius Press, 2005)

Epilog (Einsiedeln: Johannes Verlag, 1987)
ET *Epilogue*, tr. Adrian J. Walker (San Francisco: Ignatius Press, 1991)

2. Other Works of von Balthasar Referred to

The Theology of Karl Barth: Exposition and Interpretation, tr. Edward T. Oakes (San Francisco: Ignatius Press, 1992) originally *Karl Barth: Darstellung und Deutung seiner Theologie* (Cologne: Verlag Jakob Hegner, 1951)
Love Alone: The Way of Revelation, (London: Sheed & Ward, 1968) originally *Glaubhaft ist nur Liebe* (Einsiedeln: Johannes Verlag, 1963), recently re-issued in a new translation by D.C. Schindler, *Love Alone is Credible* (San Francisco: Ignatius Press, 2004)
First Glance at Adrienne von Speyr, tr. Antje Lawry and Sergia Englund (San Francisco: Ignatius Press, 1981) originally *Erster Blick auf Adrienne von Speyr* (Einsiedeln: Johannes Verlag, 1968)
'In Retrospect', *Communio: International Catholic Review*, 1975 included in (ed.) Riches, *The Analogy of Beauty: The Theology of Hans Urs von Balthasar* (Edinburgh: T&T Clark, 1986) pp. 194–221; originally *Rechenschaft 1965* (Einsiedeln: Johannes Verlag, 1965)
Mysterium Paschale: The Mystery of Easter, tr. Aidan Nichols (Edinburgh: T&T Clark, 1990) originally *Theologie der drei Tage* (Einsiedeln: Benziger, 1969)

SECONDARY SOURCES

Bieler, Martin, 'Meta-anthropology and Christology: On the Philosophy of Hans Urs von Balthasar', in *Communio: International Catholic Review*, Vol. XX No.1, (1993) 129–46
Block, Ed. Jr., (ed.) *Glory, Grace and Culture: The Work of Hans Urs von Balthasar* (New Jersey: Paulist Press, 2005
Carabine, Deirdre, 'The Fathers: The Church's Intimate Youthful Diary', in (eds) McGregor and Norris, *The Beauty of Christ: An Introduction to the Theology of Hans Urs von Balthasar* (Edinburgh: T&T Clark, 1994) pp. 73–91

Chapp, Larry, 'Revelation', in (eds) Oakes and Moss, *The Cambridge Companion to Hans Urs von Balthasar* (Cambridge: Cambridge University Press, 2004) pp. 11–23

Chia, Roland, *Revelation and Theology: The Knowledge of God in Balthasar and Barth* (Berne: Peter Lang, 1999)

Crammer, Corinne, 'One Sex or Two? Balthasar's Theology of the Sexes', in (eds) Oakes and Moss, *The Cambridge Companion to Hans Urs von Balthasar* (Cambridge: Cambridge University Press, 2004) pp. 93–112

Dalzell, Thomas G., *The Dramatic Encounter of Divine and Human Freedom in the Theology of Hans Urs von Balthasar* (Berne: Peter Lang, 2000)

Davies, Oliver, 'The Theological Aesthetics', in (eds) Oakes and Moss, *The Cambridge Companion to Hans Urs von Balthasar* (Cambridge: Cambridge University Press, 2004) pp. 131–42

Dickens, W. T., *Hans Urs von Balthasar's Theological Aesthetics: A Model for Post-Critical Interpretation* (Indiana: University of Notre Dame Press, 2003)

Henrici, Peter, 'Hans Urs von Balthasar: A Sketch of His Life' and 'The Philosophy of Hans Urs von Balthasar', in (ed.) David L. Schindler, *Hans Urs von Balthasar: His Life and Work* (San Francisco: Ignatius Press, 1991) pp. 7–43 and pp. 149–67

—, 'Hans Urs von Balthasar: His Cultural and Theological Education', in (eds) McGregor and Norris, *The Beauty of Christ: An Introduction to the Theology of Hans Urs von Balthasar* (Edinburgh: T&T Clark, 1994) pp. 10–22

Gardner, Lucy, Moss, David, Quash, Ben and Ward, Graham (eds) *Balthasar at the End of Modernity* (Edinburgh: T&T Clark, 1999)

Gavronski, Raymond, *Word and Silence: Hans Urs von Balthasar and the Spiritual Encounter between East and West* (Edinburgh: T&T Clark, 1995)

Healy, Nicholas J., *The Eschatology of Hans Urs von Balthasar: Being as Communion* (Oxford: Oxford University Press, 2005)

Howsare, Rodney, *Hans Urs von Balthasar and Protestantism: The Ecumenical Implications of his Theological Style* (London/New York: T&T Clark Int'l., 2005)

—, *Balthasar: A Guide for the Perplexed* (London/New York: T&T Clark Int'l., 2009)

Kehl, Medard, 'Hans Urs von Balthasar: A Portrait', in (eds) Medard and Löser, (trs) Robert J. Daley and Fred Lawrence, *The von Balthasar Reader* (1980) (Edinburgh: T&T Clark, 1982) pp. 3–54

Kerr, Fergus,'Foreword: Assessing this 'Giddy Synthesis', in (eds) Gardner, Moss, Quash and Ward, *Balthasar at the End of Modernity* (Edinburgh: T&T Clark, 1999) pp. 1–13

Kilby, Karen, 'Balthasar and Karl Rahner', in (eds) Oakes and Moss, *The Cambridge Companion to Hans Urs von Balthasar* (Cambridge: Cambridge University Press, 2004) pp. 256–68

Leahy, Brendan, 'Theological Aesthetics', in (eds) McGregor and Norris, *The Beauty of Christ: An Introduction to the Theology of Hans Urs von Balthasar* (Edinburgh: T&T Clark, 1994) pp. 23–55

de Lubac, Henri, *The Discovery of God* (1956) tr. Alexander Dru (Edinburgh: T & T Clark, 1986)

McGregor, Bede, and Norris, Thomas (eds) *The Beauty of Christ: An Introduction to the Theology of Hans Urs von Balthasar* (Edinburgh: T&T Clark, 1994)

McIntosh, Mark A., *Christology from Within: Spirituality and the Incarnation in Hans Urs von Balthasar* (Notre Dame: University of Notre Dame Press, 2000)

MacKinnon, Donald, 'Some Reflections on Hans Urs von Balthasar's Christology with Special Reference to *Theodramatik* II/2 and III', in (ed.) Riches, *The Analogy of Beauty: The Theology of Hans Urs von Balthasar* (Edinburgh: T&T Clark, 1986) pp. 164–79

Mongrain, Kevin, *The Systematic Thought of Hans Urs von Balthasar: An Irenaean Retrieval* (New York: Herder & Herder, 2002)

Nichols, Aidan, 'An Introduction to Balthasar', *New Blackfriars*, Vol. 79 No.923 (1998) 2–10

—, *The Word Has Been Abroad: A Guide through Balthasar's Aesthetics*, (Edinburgh: T&T Clark, 1998)

—, *No Bloodless Myth: A Guide through Balthasar's Dramatics* (Edinburgh: T&T Clark, 2000)

—, *Say It Is Pentecost: A Guide through Balthasar's Logic* (Edinburgh: T&T Clark, 2001)

Oakes, Edward T., *Pattern of Redemption: The Theology of Hans Urs von Balthasar* (New York: Continuum, 1994)

Oakes, Edward T. and Moss, David (eds) *The Cambridge Companion to Hans Urs von Balthasar* (Cambridge: Cambridge University Press, 2004)

O'Donoghue, Noel, 'A Theology of Beauty', in (ed.) Riches, *The Analogy of Beauty: The Theology of Hans Urs von Balthasar* (Edinburgh: T&T Clark, 1986) pp. 1–10

—, 'Do We Get Beyond Plato? A Critical Appreciation of the Theological Aesthetics', in (eds) McGregor and Norris, *The Beauty of Christ: An Introduction to the Theology of Hans Urs von Balthasar'* (Edinburgh: T&T Clark, 1994) pp. 253–66

O'Donnell, John, *Hans Urs von Balthasar* (London: Chapman, 1992)

O'Hanlon, Gerard, *The Immutability of God in the Theology of Hans Urs von Balthasar* (Cambridge: Cambridge University Press, 1990)

—, 'Theological Dramatics', in (eds) McGregor and Norris, *The Beauty of Christ: An Introduction to the Theology of Hans Urs von Balthasar* (Edinburgh: T&T Clark, 1994) pp. 92–111

Quash, Ben, 'Von Balthasar and the Dialogue with Karl Barth', *New Blackfriars*, Vol. 79 No. 923, 1998) pp. 45–55

—, 'The Theo-Drama', in (eds) Oakes and Moss, *The Cambridge Companion to Hans Urs von Balthasar* (Cambridge: Cambridge University Press, 2004) pp. 143–57

—, *Theology and the Drama of History* (Cambridge: Cambridge University Press, 2005)

Riches, John, (ed.) *The Analogy of Beauty: The Theology of Hans Urs von Balthasar* (Edinburgh: T&T Clark, 1986)

Riches, John, 'Hans Urs von Balthasar', in (ed.) Ford, David, *The Modern Theologians* Vol. I, (Oxford: Blackwell, 1989) pp. 237–54

Roberts, Louis, *The Theological Aesthetics of Hans Urs von Balthasar* (Washington: Catholic University of America Press, 1987)

Schindler, David L., (ed.) *Hans Urs von Balthasar: His Life and Work* (San Francisco: Ignatius Press, 1991)

Schindler, D. C., *Hans Urs von Balthasar and the Dramatic Structure of Truth* (New York: Fordham University Press, 2004)

Scola, Angelo, *Hans Urs von Balthasar: A Theological Style* (1991) ET (Grand Rapids, MI: Eerdmans, 1995)

Sherry, Patrick, *Spirit and Beauty: An Introduction to Theological Aesthetics*, 2nd edn. (London: SCM, 2002)

Thompson, John, 'Barth and Balthasar: An Ecumenical Dialogue', in (eds) McGregor and Norris, *The Beauty of Christ: An Introduction to the Theology of Hans Urs von Balthasar* (Edinburgh: T&T Clark, 1994) pp. 171–92

Viladesau, Richard, *Theological Aesthetics: God in Imagination, Beauty and Art* (New York: Oxford University Press, 1999)

Wainwright, Geoffrey, 'Eschatology', in (eds) Oakes and Moss, *The Cambridge Guide to von Balthasar* (Cambridge: Cambridge University Press, 2004) pp. 113–127

Webster, John, 'Balthasar and Karl Barth', in (eds) Oakes and Moss, *The Cambridge Companion to Hans Urs von Balthasar* (Cambridge: Cambridge University Press, 2004) pp. 241–55

Wigley, Stephen, *Karl Barth and Hans Urs von Balthasar: A Critical Engagement* (London/New York: T&T Clark Int'l, 2007)

Williams, Rowan, 'Balthasar and Rahner', in (ed.) Riches, *The Analogy of Beauty: The Theology of Hans Urs von Balthasar* (Edinburgh: T&T Clark, 1986) pp. 11–34

—, 'Afterword: Making Differences' in (eds) Gardner, Moss, Quash and Ward *Balthasar at the End of Modernity* (Edinburgh: T&T Clark, 1999) pp. 173–79

INDEX